Praise for
BELIEVING AND ITS TENSIONS

"A theological confession of the author's struggle
with serious religious conflicts and his innovative
resolutions. Neil Gillman spreads a wide pluralistic net
that captures the polarities of Jewish temperament and
proposes paths to their reconciliation."

—Rabbi Harold M. Schulweis,
Valley Beth Shalom, Encino, California; author,
Conscience: The Duty to Obey and the Duty to Disobey

"A work of profound clarity and courage. Very rarely
does a theologian of such stature have the capacity to
teach the methodology of intellectual creativity and
reflection. If the present generation is wise and brave,
it will study Gillman as a model and as a path."

—Rabbi Rachel Sabath Beit-Halachmi, PhD,
Shalom Hartman Institute

"With his mind focused unerringly on the great
theological questions, the latest work by Neil Gillman
is concise, incisive, bold and delightful. He tells his
readers where he now stands and challenges us to
stretch our imaginations to span Heschel and the
Higgs boson, John Donne and Elie Wiesel. Many
thinkers take five times longer to say half as much. We
are lucky to have Neil Gillman!"

—Rabbi Michael Marmur, PhD, assistant professor of
Jewish theology and vice president for academic affairs,
Hebrew Union College–Jewish Institute of Religion

"Gut-check time for the religiously serious reader! With faith and courageous honesty, Gillman examines the limits of theological certainty. God, of course, and also suffering and death must ever remain beyond our ability to understand fully."

—**Rabbi Ralph D. Mecklenburger**,
Beth-El Congregation, Fort Worth, Texas;
author, *Our Religious Brains: What Cognitive Science Reveals about Belief, Morality, Community and Our Relationship with God*

"A model of honesty and courage in theological quest. Gillman reminds us that living with tensions makes us grow and stretch. May the God he questions give him strength to go forward with his challenge!"

—**Arthur Green**, rector, Rabbinical School, Hebrew College;
author, *Seek My Face: A Jewish Mystical Theology*

"If his best-known works are theological treatises, this book is a public offering of Neil Gillman's unfolding conversation with himself and his students. It reflects his uncanny and disarming ability to 'translate' big ideas into story, anecdote and personal reflection."

—**Rabbi Leon Morris**, rabbi, Temple Adas Israel, Sag Harbor, New York; former director, Skirball Center for Adult Jewish Learning at Temple Emanu-El

"In this rich distillation of decades of teaching, scholarly research and personal exploration, Neil Gillman addresses issues of ultimate meaning. He engages readers with a highly sophisticated, lucid, accessible and concise articulation of his personal theology and its development, while challenging them to think and rethink their own. A must read!"

—**Dr. Anne Lapidus Lerner**, former vice chancellor,
The Jewish Theological Seminary;
author, *Eternally Eve: Images of Eve in the Hebrew Bible, Midrash and Modern Jewish Poetry*

"Honest, informed, intelligent, wise, clear, open and personal—these are rare qualities for a book on theology, but Neil Gillman's new book is all of those. Moreover, he calls on what he learns not only from philosophy and the Jewish tradition, but also from neuroscience, anthropology and sociology. Readers will not necessarily agree with all of Gillman's views, but one cannot read this book without being challenged to confront one's own faith with equal knowledge, clarity and honesty. This book is thus an important contribution to the thinking of each and every one of us."

—**Rabbi Elliot N. Dorff, PhD**, rector and professor of philosophy, American Jewish University; author, *Knowing God: Jewish Journeys to the Unknowable* and *The Way Into* Tikkun Olam *(Repairing the World)*

Believing
and Its
Tensions

Believing
and Its
Tensions

*A Personal Conversation
about God, Torah,
Suffering and Death
in Jewish Thought*

Rabbi Neil Gillman, PhD

For People of All Faiths, All Backgrounds

JEWISH LIGHTS Publishing

Woodstock, Vermont

Believing and Its Tensions:
A Personal Conversation about God, Torah, Suffering and Death
in Jewish Thought

2013 Hardcover Edition, First Printing
© 2013 by Neil Gillman

For information regarding permission to reprint material from this book, please write or fax your request to Jewish Lights Publishing, Permissions Department, at the address / fax number listed below, or e-mail your request to permissions@jewishlights.com.

Grateful acknowledgment is given for permission to use "And Death Shall Have No Dominion," by Dylan Thomas, from *The Poems of Dylan Thomas*, copyright © 1943 by New Directions Publishing Corps. Reprinted with permission of New Directions Publishing Corps.

Library of Congress Cataloging-in-Publication Data
Gillman, Neil.
Believing and its tensions : a personal conversation about God, Torah, suffering and death in Jewish thought / Rabbi Neil Gillman, PhD.
     pages cm
  Includes bibliographical references.
  ISBN 978-1-58023-669-0
  1. Faith (Judaism) 2. Judaism—Doctrines. I. Title.
  BM729.F3G55 2013
  296.3—dc23
                                        2013012857

10 9 8 7 6 5 4 3 2 1

Manufactured in the United States of America
Jacket Design: Tim Holtz
Cover Art: © Color Symphony/Shutterstock.com

For People of All Faiths, All Backgrounds
Jewish Lights Publishing
A Division of LongHill Partners, Inc.
Sunset Farm Offices, Route 4, P.O. Box 237
Woodstock, VT 05091
Tel: (802) 457-4000   Fax: (802) 457-4004
www.jewishlights.com

For Nava Gillman Kass

הַרְאִינִי אֶת־מַרְאַיִךְ
הַשְׁמִיעִנִי אֶת־קוֹלֵךְ
כִּי־קוֹלֵךְ עָרֵב וּמַרְאֵיךְ נָאוֶה

Let me view your countenance,
Let me hear your voice;
For your voice is sweet
Your countenance, comely.
—SONG OF SONGS 2:14

Contents

Preface

The original inspiration for this book was a brief conversation with the then managing editor of the periodical *Conservative Judaism*. The conversation coincided with my decision to retire from teaching at The Jewish Theological Seminary after a career of just about fifty years as a member and ultimately the chairman of the Department of Jewish Philosophy. I was then in my midseventies and was tiring of the rounds of classroom activity, faculty committee meetings, the submitting of syllabi, and the grading of papers. I had always enjoyed an active role in publishing and in adult education programs around the country.

My colleague's suggestion was that I owed my students at the Seminary and elsewhere a summary statement of my theological legacy. I had published a number of shorter papers and had been lecturing on what I considered to be the central theological issues of the day. But since my original publication, *Sacred Fragments: Recovering Theology for the Modern Jew* (1990), I had not published a summary statement of where I stood on the wide range of issues that Jewish theologians have dealt with over the past centuries.

To my astonishment, *Sacred Fragments* continued to be my personal best seller, and upon rereading it, I discovered how much it still reflected both my current thinking some twenty years later and my more recent thinking on central issues. I resolved then that if I followed my colleague's advice, I would write a much shorter book that would concentrate on the issues on which my thinking has changed and the extent to which this change reflected my ongoing teaching and lecturing in the past decade. The book would deal with four issues: God, revelation, suffering, and death.

The original problem that I encountered was that until this conversation, I had been resolved to work on an anthology of commentaries on the biblical story of the *akedah*, Binding of Isaac, modeled somewhat on Nahum Glatzer's *Dimensions of Job*. I had been teaching full-semester courses on the *akedah* and its interpretations and had accumulated a good deal of midrashic, philosophical, interreligious, and general humanistic explications of this enigmatic story. I had quickly realized that there was no single anthology of this material.

I had enlisted the help of two student research assistants in thinking through how to organize that material, and I had even obtained a preliminary consent from my publisher, Jewish Lights, to publish that book as well.

It was clear to me, however, that I could not work on both books at the same time. The more I reflected on my immediate priorities, the more intrigued I was by the idea of working first on my theological legacy. In order to free myself to do this, I engaged one of my former research assistants, Rabbi Noah Farkas, now a congregational rabbi in California, to concentrate on the *akedah* book with my assistance and support, while I worked on the theology book. Jewish Lights agreed with this proposal.

To my dismay, as I began to outline the new book, I became ill, and I have since endured two bouts of struggling with cancer, the first involving surgery and radiation and the second involving extensive chemotherapy—both demanding significant expenditures of time and energy.

I determined, however, that the theology book should be completed, and although I could not work on the computer, I could easily dictate the contents of the four main chapters, because I had been teaching this material and lecturing on the road. The idiom that I was using to convey this material was very fresh in my mind and in my mouth, so it could easily be dictated and ultimately transcribed into print. The print version could then be edited. The result is what you have before you. I am particularly grateful to Emily Wichland of Jewish Lights for the grace and thoroughness with which she guided my manuscript into print.

I should emphasize that this is hardly a revision of *Sacred Fragments*. It certainly is an updating and, I believe, a much more forthright, maybe even controversial, statement of my current views. I also aimed to write a much more colloquial statement, considerably more concise and omitting the extensive argumentation and justification for my current conclusions. A brief bibliography directs the reader to the books that have influenced me. The views expressed here represent my conclusions to date. None of us can ever be certain of what lies ahead, and conceivably—maybe even desirably—my thinking will continue to evolve. Of course, at this stage of my life, there are no guarantees.

Since my retirement from active teaching at the Seminary, I have found an alternative home with the Skirball Center for Adult Jewish Learning at Temple Emanu-El in New York City. Skirball has provided me with a new community of students who are eager to delve into theological issues. I am grateful to Rabbi Alfredo Borodofsky and Rabbi Yael Smilowitz for having provided me with these new opportunities to teach.

I am also grateful to the members of what we have come to call the Ostow Seminar. This workshop was created decades ago by my late teacher and then colleague Dr. Mortimer Ostow, a prominent psychiatrist, psychoanalyst, and committed Conservative

Jew. Morty suggested that he and I cochair a discussion group composed of psychotherapists and Jewish Theological Seminary faculty to discuss the psychological effects of Jewish liturgy and worship. This group continued to meet even after Morty's death, and the topics of discussion have moved far away from the original intent. But our further discussions, often bearing on neuroscience and religion, are reflected in the pages of this book. I am grateful for the group's continued interest and commitment to our study experience.

When I began to publish books, I resolved to dedicate them to members of my family. I have followed this procedure except for once, when I dedicated my study of Conservative Judaism to my students at the Seminary and elsewhere. However, there are dedicatory statements in all of my other books to my wife Sarah, to my daughters and sons-in-law, and to four of my grandchildren. Now God has graced me with a new granddaughter, born on *erev* Yom Kippur three years ago. Her birth has undoubtedly helped to serve as the conscious or unconscious inspiration to publish another book, which is therefore dedicated to her, Nava Gillman Kass. She is, providentially, filled with the kind of spirit, courage, and forthrightness in her personality that I hope you will find embodied in these theological statements.

My wife and daughters have been sources of support beyond measure during the course of my recent illness. They have made possible my survival.

I must also express my gratitude to two research assistants, Nina Kretzmer and Gella Solomon, both of whom are totally familiar with all of the twists and turns of my thinking over the past years, and both of whom contributed to getting the oral version of this book into print. But most of all, I am grateful to my son-in-law, Professor Michael Prince of Boston University, who, working from past drafts, produced the version that is largely the basis for this published book. That effort, at a time when I was most dependent on the help of others, was simply indispensable. I thank him for this splendid act of generosity.

CHAPTER 1

God

Several months ago I was invited to discuss theology with a fourth-grade class in a neighboring Jewish day school. I came into a classroom with fourteen young boys and girls. As I typically do in these kinds of settings, after introducing myself and asking them to introduce themselves to me, I asked them to write down what they sense, feel, and visualize whenever they use the term *God*—to write it or to draw it, if they wished, and then to hand it to me. I gave them about ten minutes, with the students in a circle around me, then I collected the papers and began to review them. I suggested that some of them allow me to read what they had written to the rest of the group; if they did not want me to, however, I would respect their wishes.

On the top of the pile of papers in my hand, I saw the following statement: "When I visualize God, He looks like a blob. God can shift into everything, anything He wants."

There followed a drawing of a shapeless creature of some kind, with legs and arms in all directions and a tortured-looking face, with two dots for eyes. What this young girl called a blob, I would have called, recalling my early childhood interest in the *Li'l Abner* comics, a *Shmoo*. The Shmoo has the quality of being able to adapt to whatever the owner wishes. If you would like a steak, the Shmoo becomes a steak. If you'd like a house, the Shmoo becomes a house. The Shmoo, as you can imagine, is a valuable creature. This blob looked very much like Li'l Abner's Shmoo. The sentence that stood out for me was "God can shift into everything He wants," and when I pushed her on this sentence, the girl said, "Really what I meant was that God can shift into anything I want or we want." In a very unsophisticated kind of way, what this young girl was articulating was a highly sophisticated understanding of the nature of God, a view of God as very much the product of our own subjective needs.

God can, in effect, be whatever we envision God to be. This accounts for the various images of God that many of us continue to use in order to worship and to ground our theology. That this girl was in fourth grade stunned me, because I, in my own development, did not have any kind of image of

God, serious or not, until I reached my latter years in college. Since then, of course, my image of God has changed in many different ways to become what it is today, but if you had asked me at that stage in my life, or even later in my early education, how I visualized God, I would have been shocked by the question. I probably would have come up with a very primitive notion of an old man with a long beard in a white robe seated in a chair up in the sky.

THE GOD BEYOND VERSUS THE GOD OF EVERYDAY EXPERIENCE

If I were to try to characterize the evolution of my thinking about religion in general and even specifically about God, I would say that I find an expanding tendency toward naturalism. Naturalism here is in contrast to supernaturalism. *Supernaturalism* suggests that religion and God occupy a realm beyond the natural, beyond the world as we know it, and we can talk about it beyond the familiar everyday world of our existence, even though that realm is unfamiliar. *Naturalism*, in contrast, views religion as originating from and dealing with issues that are very much within the world of our experience. A supernaturalist God, then, is essentially beyond ourselves, but a naturalist God is very much involved with, characterized by, or part of the familiar world of our everyday experience. My religious outlook and my theology have evolved from a traditionalist supernaturalism of my more childish years, from my early education until the middle of my undergraduate career. Only then did I first begin to think seriously about philosophical and theological issues.

Since then, in a series of graduated steps, my thinking on a variety of issues has moved away from that supernaturalism and toward a much more naturalist understanding. The first step, as I shall detail in the next chapter, probably occurred when I was in rabbinical school. I gradually learned that none of my teachers, and certainly none of my colleagues, believed that the story of the revelation of the Torah, as it is composed and recorded in chapters 19 and 20 of the book of Exodus, is an accurate historical, literal account of what actually happened some thousands of years ago in the Sinai desert. Although my teachers didn't discuss their opinions overtly, they certainly suggested that the account in Exodus was a folktale— or as I later called it, a myth. It certainly was not history to them.

> The LORD came down upon Mount Sinai, to the top of the mountain, and the LORD called Moses to the top of the mountain and Moses went up. The LORD said to Moses, "Go down, warn the people not to break through to the LORD to gaze, lest many will perish. The priests also, who come near the LORD, must stay pure, lest the LORD will break out against them."

> But Moses said to the LORD, "The
> people cannot come up to Mount Sinai;
> for You warned us, saying, 'Set bounds
> about the mountain and sanctify it.'" So
> the LORD said to him, "Go down, and
> come back together with Aaron; but let
> not the priests or the people break through
> to come up to the LORD, lest He break
> out against them." And Moses went down
> to the people and told them.
>
> (EXODUS 19:20–25)

The notion of a God from beyond descending onto
the mountaintop and speaking Hebrew words to our
ancestors was simply incompatible with their ability
to think about God, history, and the origins of religion. That was, of course, a supernaturalist understanding of revelation.

Eventually, the supernaturalist notion was
replaced in my own mind with a more naturalist
understanding of the origins of the Torah and the
Jewish religion: Judaism as a religion emerged from
the communal experience of my ancestors, a human
community, and the attribution of the content of the
Torah to the words of a God who is beyond the natural order was a later attempt to establish the authority of the text, of this God, and of Judaism. I didn't
appreciate at that point how monumental and revolutionary this epiphany was for me, but of course
it changed everything. If the Torah is a product of

human experience, then the authority of the Torah changed from a supernatural being, God, to the community itself. What of course follows is that whatever a human community designates as the Torah is open to reconsideration as the community moves through history. Effectively, it is the Jewish people who created the Torah and with it everything that we call Judaism, the Jewish religion, and tradition.

This change of view was an early step in the evolution of my religious outlook from supernaturalism to naturalism. It then moved into other areas—for example, into the area of ritual. When I began to study religious anthropology, psychology, and sociology, I learned that every community has both rituals of its own and rituals that are developed with experience. If the authority of a supernatural God no longer dictated to me the dietary laws, festivals, daily prayers, and other rituals that to this day make up my life experience as a Jew, then where did these rituals come from? The alternative theory was that the rituals emerged from the life experience of a community—hence a naturalist understanding of ritual: communities, out of similar needs, create various rituals to fill them. I then became interested in eschatology and wrote *The Death of Death: Resurrection and Immortality in Jewish Thought*, a book about the afterlife. It occurred to me that theologies of resurrection, life after death, and immortality serve as a response to historical and human conditions, just like other rituals do—hence a naturalist approach to eschatology.

DISCOVERING GOD BY
INVENTING WORD PICTURES

The latest and most difficult step in my evolving religious naturalism had to do with God. My own thinking proceeded through a series of epiphanies, each of which took a number of years, much thinking, and much reading before it became a firmly held conviction of mine.

First, the notion that the Torah itself was the creation of a community of human beings suggested to me right away that God, or the images and portraits of God that occurred throughout the pages of the Torah—what I later came to call "word pictures"— were in fact also the creation of a human community. It was the human community that placed God into the Torah. Just as the community placed in the Torah the rituals and the historical narratives that I now understood to be folktales, legends, and myths, so too did it locate God in various changing guises as the main character in this extensive, rich, and fascinating historical drama. God is in the Torah because the people who conceived of the Torah in the first place made God the primary actor in the story of how they themselves came to be.

When I suggested this to my students, their immediate question was "So, Professor Gillman, do we discover God or invent God?" My off-the-cuff answer—which I'm convinced is accurate, although it requires elaboration—is that we discover God, but we invent the images of God. We discover God in our experience of the world—not through miracles, not through sudden revelations from mountaintops, but from the everyday experience of God's presence in our lives, in history, and in nature.

But simply to discover God raises a host of problems: How do we know it's God? Why do we identify whatever it is we experience as God? How do we tie this God to the God of our people's historical experience? At that point it seemed to me that all of our images of God were metaphors. This is when I began using the term *metaphor*. A metaphor is, of course, a literary device in which, as the literal meaning of the Greek term suggests, we carry over the use of a characterization from a familiar location to a less familiar location. Because the two objects to be compared are similar enough that they convey the same image, they create the same emotion. One could say, for example, that the lion is the king of the beasts, that General Motors shrugged off a dip in the stock market, or that one's refrigerator is running.

So what the Bible and all of Jewish theological writing throughout postrabbinical literature present us with is page after page of metaphors in which God appears as a king, a judge, a shepherd, a lover, a parent with a rich emotional life, and sometimes a tyrant. This God can be pleased or angry, and can cry, rejoice, or punish. This is what my teacher and late colleague Yochanan Muffs dubbed the "personhood of God." God emerges in all of our traditional texts as a very rich, interesting, and humanlike character, sometimes in the first person:

> *Because he is devoted to Me, I will*
> *   deliver him;*
> *I will keep him safe, for he knows*
> *   My name.*
> *When he calls upon Me, I will*
> *   answer him;*
> *I will be with him in distress,*
> *I will rescue him and make him*
> *   honored;*
> *I will let him live to a ripe old age*
> *and show him My salvation.*
>
> (PSALM 91:14–16)

In effect, we can call all of Jewish religious thinking a treasure chest of metaphors. Metaphor enables us to see the unseen, hear the unheard, and grasp the ungraspable. When we come to our experience with a metaphor of God as a particular characterization, such as our lover, we tend to want to experience God as that characterization; we soon forget that it's a metaphor, and God simply becomes literally—almost objectively—our lover, a tyrant, our judge, a mourner, pleased, angry, punitive, or any of the other characterizations of God in our tradition and our liturgy.

I later dropped the term *metaphor* because I thought that it was tied too much to literary usage. What I wanted to suggest was something infinitely richer than a simple literary device. So I began to adopt the possibly more effective term *word picture*, although I immediately had to add the proviso that our ancestors believed that they were not permitted to make pictures of God. Yet even though they had this prohibition, they painted marvelous mental images of God through language. Jews didn't draw pictures of God, but we carved out images of God in words. My student in fourth grade, for example, wrote an image of God in words: "a blob." She then, on her own, drew a picture of the blob that she conceived God to be.

At a later stage of inquiry, I began to ask myself, "So where did this treasure chest of metaphors come from?" Where did our ancestors pick up the various characterizations of God that they wove into biblical, midrashic, and liturgical texts and made part of our everyday lives as Jews? The only answer I could possibly come up with was that these word pictures emerged because our ancestors looked at the most immediate source of information about what God must be like. That is, they looked in a mirror (or, before mirrors, in a body of water), in which they saw represented the totality of their human experience. There's no other way of accounting for the "personhood of God," the way in which God appears in such a human guise throughout these texts. My sense is that God emerges very much as a person with all of the characteristics of a person and with all of the accomplishments, failings, ups and downs, and tensions that accompany a human life. Where did these human guises or images come from if not from the very sophisticated self-awareness that our ancestors had of themselves as human beings? Did our ancestors invent this God? Was God a product of their imaginations? Is God a fiction? My answer is no. My sense is that they lived with an experience of God's presence in their day-to-day lives and in their attempts to understand what the world was all about and what a human life meant. In that experience, they came across this multifaceted God, which they then incorporated into their thinking and into their texts.

There is no question, then, of the subjective quality of all human thinking about God. There is no underestimating the revolutionary nature of this gradual awareness of the true nature of all religious claims. It requires pluralism—not only among different human beings who have different and equally subjective experiences of God that lead to different word pictures, but also among the many and often contradictory, shifting images of God that occur in our texts. The Bible was canonized, which means that the text as it was received became fixed and authoritative, but it is in fact the product of different communities at different times composed by different individuals, each recording the experience of God and the word pictures of God that emerge from these experiences. So it is pluralistic not only in terms of the human community but also in the way in which God was conceived by various communities in their specific contexts.

Along with subjectivity comes the notion that all religious and theological claims have to be understood as provisional. Nothing is objective, true, or fixed forever. We can read the Bible as a story of the evolution of these images of God because none of the images is ever completely constant. The God of the Genesis stories, for example, is very different from the God of the prophets; or, as I have frequently taught, the God of Chanukah is very different from the God of Passover, the God of Tisha B'Av, or the God of Yom Kippur. Whether a warrior, a punitive God, a consoling God, or a judging God, these different images are all equally provisional in the sense that they apply to certain aspects of our life experiences. The word picture fortifies or canonizes each of these images. The creation of these images is potentially a subjective, provisional, elaborate, changing system, subject only to the authority dictated by an established clergy or a rabbi who is prepared to dictate and require commitment to a specific series of theological claims. Christianity has its creeds, its Credo, and its catechism. Judaism has Maimonides's Code of Law, which includes a theological preface that also claims that all references to God are metaphors. In the first pages of Maimonides's Code you find:

Moses our Teacher himself saw Him at the Red Sea as a mighty man waging war (Ex. 15:3) and on Sinai, as a congregational reader wrapped (in his tallit)—all indicating that in reality He has no form or figure. These only appeared in a prophetic vision. But God's essence as it really is, the human mind does not understand and is incapable of grasping or investigating.... This being so, the expressions in the Pentateuch and the books of the Prophets already mentioned, and others similar to these, are all of them metaphorical and rhetorical, as for example, "He that sits in the heavens shall laugh" (Ps. 2:4), "They have provoked Me to anger with their vanities" (Deut. 32:21), "As the Lord rejoiced" (ibid. 28:63), etc. To all these phrases applies the saying "The Torah speaks in the language of men."[1]

RELIGION AND
THE BRAIN

My ophthalmologist once told me in the midst of an examination that we see with our brains and not with our eyes. Seeing is a very complicated process. What we perceive through eyesight is only the very beginning of a much more complicated human experience that involves many different aspects of our brains and of our identities, such as our education level, our race, and our gender, all of which influence us in a split second. In a sense, I *experience* God rather than *see* God. That experience is as much the work of our brains and our hearts as it is of our eyes. There is a whole series of neurological assumptions that lead us to understand that our experience of the world is highly interpretive; therefore, there is very little about which we can say that our experience of God is objectively accurate. We don't have an objective image of God. We have an interpretive, subjective experience. We can still work in a community because there is enough commonality among the members. Our traditional texts also serve as a source of communal unity, so we tend to want to drift into communal experiences, which themselves lead to communal images of God. That's why we have a Bible, rabbinic literature, and prayer books.

A further word about neuroscience: I first became interested in neuroscience when I was working on *The Death of Death*, my book on the afterlife that deals with the immortality of the soul. This got me involved in the whole attempt to understand the differences among brain, mind, and soul. What is the soul? Is the soul the same thing as the mind? In what way is the mind different from the brain? Is the brain something I can hold in my hand, whereas the mind cannot be held in the hand? In a television interview with Eric Kandel, the eminent Nobel Prize–winning neuroscientist, the interviewer asked what the difference is between the mind and the brain. Kandel replied, "Mind is what the brain does."[2] *Brain* is a noun, an object, whereas *mind* is a verb, a process or an activity.

In another interview, Kandel suggested that we are entering the century of neuroscience and that specific branches of neuroscience would soon develop. He talked about neuroethics and neuro-aesthetics. Add neurotheology, I thought. Because the brain is involved in everything that we do, our attempt to deal with theological issues such as God also involves the brain and brain activity. I was very much interested in trying to study what happens in the brain when we think about God. But is this satis-fying? Is it the case that when I think about God, all that's happening are certain processes and activities in my brain? I recall mentioning to the father of a student of mine, himself a neuroscientist, "It's hard for me to conceive of the fact that when I think of God, all that's involved is a series of neurons firing in my brain." He smiled, looked at me, and said, "Professor Gillman, sorry, but that's all there is." I winced and replied, "Well, I hope that there is more to it than that."

> *Brain is a noun, an object, whereas mind is a verb, a process or an activity.*

Of course there has to be more to it than that! Most human beings in the world since the beginning of history have thought about God, and it is inconceivable to me that all human thought about God was and is a matter of neurons flashing around in the brain in various complex interfaces. I say this knowing that this extreme neurological determinism is a logical extension of my religious naturalism. Also, it can't only be biology, because everything that takes place in the brain is affected by one's total life experience. What we see, what we feel, what we experience, our education level, our gender, and our relationships all have an effect on our brains and contribute to whatever it is that the brain works out.

FROM LITERALISM
TO MYTH

I have begun to reject a position that I took many years ago in my doctoral dissertation, which was devoted to the religious epistemology of the French Catholic existentialist philosopher Gabriel Marcel. In the course of this dissertation, I dealt with the issue of whether theological religious claims can be proven to be true or false. At that point in my thinking, I was very much inclined to try to prove that they could be. I wanted to show that there was not a significant difference between theological claims and scientific claims and that theology, of course, deals with far more subtle and complicated issues. I realize that this is no longer the case and that science deals with complex phenomena that thus far have escaped any kind of human verification or perception.

But back then I tended to be hardheaded and critical of thinkers such as Rabbi Abraham Joshua Heschel, who I felt were very soft in their analyses of theological claims. I wanted to do something much more rigorous than what they were providing. I went back to Marcel's theory of primary reflection and secondary reflection. *Primary reflection* is the kind of thinking that takes place when we first encounter the world and when we try to see everything that confronts us as problems to be solved by hardheaded scientific experimentation and rationalization. *Secondary reflection*, in contrast, is a kind of retroactive thinking in which we go back and confront the original experience, which we tried to analyze in hardheaded terms, and just allow it to be. We accept it as a more poetic, subjective, and imaginative truth that is not congenial to any hardheaded, scientific, or experimental verification. It is a different kind of brain activity that deals with the various aspects of our experience that are not subject to objective truth or falsity, but only to a more mythical kind of truth. When we deal with theological claims and religious claims, we actually invoke this kind of reflection.

I later went back to Heschel and discovered that my earlier criticism of him was misplaced. In effect, Heschel was talking about the fact that all of theology, to him, was what Marcel called secondary reflection. Heschel did not believe that science, scientific thinking, or hardheaded experimentation could yield religious or theological truth. He believed that the purpose of theology was evocative: to teach us how to see, feel, and experience the world and possibly then to experience God. This justified his writing being poetic, midrashic, and filled with feelings, which of course led to his notion of divine pathos.

Yet we are simultaneously capable of both scientific and mythical thinking. A psychiatrist with whom I work suggested that there was such a thing as right-brain and left-brain phenomena. The left hemisphere of the brain is where we deal with science and mathematical hardheaded truth; the right hemisphere of the brain is where we deal with imaginative, subjective, poetic, and artistic issues—and that's where theology really belongs. The work to be done on neurotheology is much more specific in terms of how neuroscience can help us understand theology. I am convinced that if everything that we do as human beings involves neurology and the brain, then so does theology.

We have seen theology move from literalism to secondary reflection. This is an experience that in his *Dynamics of Faith* theologian Paul Tillich called the "breaking of the myth," which simply means that a myth is recognized as myth, not as literal historical truth. The usual assumption is that once the myth is broken—namely, exposed as myth and not as fact—it doesn't work any longer. And that of course is simply not true. The myth can be remythologized and can be very much alive even though it is historically and rhetorically no longer accepted as factual. For example, I no longer believe that my ancestors were slaves in Egypt who were removed from slavery by God's intervention—which is what we celebrate at the Passover seder. But when I sit at the seder with my family, friends, and colleagues and say that we were slaves in Egypt and the Lord redeemed us from slavery, even though that is not historically

> *I am convinced that if everything that we do as human beings involves neurology and the brain, then so does theology.*

true, it nevertheless remains mythologically true, and it is true in a very different sense of truth. It still provides me with a goosebump experience as I recite those words in the context of the seder. There is a term for the revival of a myth precisely in mythical terms: *second naïveté*.

I encountered this term when I was trying to teach my rabbinical students that the biblical account of early Israelite history as recounted in the

Pentateuch was not historically true and that scholars did not accept it as historically true. Instead, it was true in a very different sense of truth. The term *second naïveté* enabled me to characterize the stage following the breaking of the myth as a legitimate epistemological stage in which one recaptures, by diverse means, the experience of the myth before the myth was broken. This was as much a matter of learning as feeling. I encountered that term for the first time in *Stages of Faith* by James Fowler. *Stages of Faith* was a very helpful book to me because it allowed me to understand my own evolution and the evolution of my students. Fowler uses stage theory, which is also used by developmental psychologist Erik Erikson in his work on psychological development, by Lawrence Kohlberg in his work on ethics, and by Swiss psychologist Jean Piaget in his work on cognitive development. The typical human being goes

> *The term* second naïveté *enabled me to characterize the stage following the breaking of the myth as a legitimate epistemological stage in which one recaptures, by diverse means, the experience of the myth before the myth was broken.*

through various stages in his or her ability to think through the data that are being presented to him or her. The stage that particularly concerns me is the one that follows the breaking of the myth: the stage that follows the exposition of the myth as precisely mythical and not literally true or historically true. This is the stage that my students are confronting all the time because when they come to rabbinical school at The Jewish Theological Seminary, they are taught that the historical account of the early experiences of the Jewish people, as recounted in the Bible, are not historically accurate. And what's left then?

I experienced primary naïveté when I was in my own pre–rabbinical school and pre–critical approach to the Torah stage, when I was with my father who accepted the whole thing as factual. I recall my own experience when that myth was broken for me, largely by Mordecai Kaplan, the founder of Reconstructionist Judaism, because it raised the whole question of why be Jewish. Why observe anything? Why take the Torah seriously? Why go to shul? Why do ritual? Why halacha, the body of Jewish law? It is here that Fowler suggests we can enter the stage of second naïveté, in which we recapture the primary naïveté we had about the myth before it was broken and recapture it with the conscious awareness that even though it might not be literally true, it can still be valuable, important, and helpful. That stage of second naïveté is what helps me reconnect with my tradition when, no matter how critically I look at it, it doesn't work. Second naïveté is the fruit of secondary reflection.

USING THE INVISIBLE
TO EXPLAIN THE VISIBLE

There are even more epistemological issues that deal with how we know there is a God or anything about this God. It is not unusual to assume that there is an invisible world that we use to explain or account for the visible world—something we do not see that helps us understand what we do see. Science does this all the time. For example, Sigmund Freud tried to understand human behavior that was very visible to him. To account for what he saw, he posited an invisible world. He called it the unconscious, and populated it with realities that he called repressed: wishes, fears, desires, memories. The unconscious is not a place. It does not fill a void in a person, but Freud used it to try to account for some of the behavior that he and others observed in human beings. He knew that this world existed because once he posited that it was there, and once he devised ways of affecting human behavior through it, it seemed to work. To him and

> *Second naïveté is the fruit of secondary reflection.*

his community of psychologists, it was useful. It had a kind of pragmatic truth to it. Even though nobody was ever able to physically put his or her finger on the unconscious—it isn't a reality in the sense that one can touch it or put it in a test tube—once Freud discovered these patterns at work in people, he was able to identify the unconscious, name it, define it. Thus it entered conversation and certain areas of psychology as science.

It is possible to say that at the outset of the human experience on Earth, there was a sense that a reality was needed that would help human beings explain why the world is as it is.

Much more recently, there was a flurry of excitement about the discovery of a cosmic particle called the Higgs boson. Here again, what preceded this discovery was a sense that something was missing in our attempt to explain the cosmos. We needed to explain the fact that our perception of how everything fits together was not adequate. The missing piece was discovered by a physicist named Professor Peter Higgs, and his discovery led to a worldwide effort to try to find this missing particle.

Most recently, that effort, conducted by numer-
ous communities of scientists, was rewarded thanks
to a supercollider in Switzerland called the Large
Hadron Collider. Within this instrument, millions
of particles were introduced and made to clash with
one another, and the resulting release of particles
could be observed. It took months to produce suf-
ficient evidence, but finally the cosmologists who
had been working on the discovery of the Higgs
boson announced triumphantly to the world that
the particle had been discovered. What did this
mean? It certainly did not mean that a miniature
Ping-Pong ball had finally been seen. The particle,
along with most subatomic particles, is not a tiny
piece of matter. Subatomic particles are rather complex activities, processes that are measured by the
computer programs that are buried deep within
the supercollider that measures the outcome of the
clashes. What scientists observe, then, is nothing
inside the supercollider, but rather a series of patterns on their computer printouts that announce
that the pattern or activity that the Higgs boson
was designed to explain is finally accessible. It was
acceptable not as a miniature reality but as a certain
pattern of activity discernible in the observation of
cosmic processes.

How did the scientists know that they had
indeed discovered this new phenomenon? When
they used it to explain a cosmic pattern, the pattern
now fit together. The classical portrait of the cosmos,

including the Higgs boson observations, explained why everything is the way it is.

The parallel with God is not identical, but it is possible to say that at the outset of the human experience on Earth, there was a sense that a reality was needed that would help human beings explain why the world is as it is. What they subsequently posited was a power or a process. Later, the projected it beyond nature, as some kind of reality—a being even—that dealt with the incompleteness and helped them understand how the world had come to be, what their place in the universe was, and what values were associated with human life. This discovery became a way of ordering the cosmos and of limiting the chaotic.

Our predecessors never observed this reality as a being, but they did have the sense that with this reality in place, they could make sense of their experience and share that with other cultures. All along they gave it an identity through a series of word pictures that seemed to account for the ways they experienced this God that they had discovered. They

> *The classical portrait of the cosmos, including the Higgs boson observations, explained why everything is the way it is.*

didn't invent God, but they did discover it, name it, and identify it in many different ways, given their many different experiences of how this God functioned in their lives. Other civilizations were doing the same thing, and this discovery was verified progressively by them as a reality, much the way that the unconscious and the Higgs boson were discovered as realities. In each case, an invisible reality was used to explain the visible world.

There are, of course, some major differences between the scientific enterprise and the religious enterprise. Scientists will claim that the Higgs boson's existence is verified by thousands of scientists observing the same computer printouts and realizing that with this new discovery in place, the world is now explicable. The discovery and subsequent identification of God was verified in ways that

> *In each case, an invisible reality was used to explain the visible world.*

were similar but not identical. We might call this a process of *soft verification*—not the hard verification that science uses to prove its discoveries, but rather a much more subjective, subtle, and emotional sense of a reality that somehow helps explain the other dimensions of the created world, such as human life, human feelings, meaning, morality, moral behavior, and, for the Jewish people, their historical experience.

THEOLOGY VALUES TENSION

Our religious outlook is subjective, provisional, and thus very tentative. This makes it necessary for us to live with a sense of tension. I confess that this contradicts one of my earlier convictions, which is that religion is basically an ordering device. The purpose of religion is to create the sense that the world is ordered, to avoid chaos, and to make sure that everything is in its proper place. That was the view of Clifford Geertz, the late anthropologist, whose paper "Religion as a Cultural System" was extremely important in the evolution of my views. As a social scientist, Geertz understood religion as an outgrowth of human communities, and communal living, which contributed to my evolving view of naturalism.

Our religious outlook is subjective, provisional, and thus very tentative. This makes it necessary for us to live with a sense of tension.

It seems to me that the major difference among religious communities today is between human beings who are comfortable with tension and human beings who require an absolute, fixed authority behind their religious beliefs.

So if religion is an ordering device, why do I sense that theology values tension? I understood this to be an outgrowth of naturalism. Human beings who have a supernaturalist understanding of religion and of God tend to view images of God and statements of God's will as objective and therefore eternally binding, totally above and beyond communal manipulation. I have rejected this notion from the moment that I stopped believing that God spoke at Sinai. If the Torah was the product of a human community, then the authority for the Torah was human, and human authority changes from generation to generation as human conditions change. If the story of religious development is subjective, tentative, and provisional, then how can it not be subject to change, and therefore how can it not be a source of tension? It seems to me that the major difference among religious communities today is between human beings who are comfortable with tension and human beings who require an absolute, fixed authority behind their religious beliefs. For the latter, nothing ever changes, because God's will supersedes all human concerns.

In working through the details of this general approach to religion and to God, I must give credit to three of my earliest theological teachers: Paul Tillich, with whom I never studied but whose writings had a major effect on me, and Mordecai Kaplan and Abraham Joshua Heschel, two of my teachers at The Jewish Theological Seminary.

Tillich was a German-born Protestant theologian who was on the forefront of religious resistance to Nazism, then came to the United States and taught at Union Theological Seminary, Harvard University, and the University of Chicago. I read his work in preparation for my doctoral examinations at Columbia University, and I have almost memorized a chapter in his slim volume *Dynamics of Faith*, which forever destroyed any hint of literalness and objectivity I had in regard to theological language. Tillich introduced me to the notion of myth that has characterized my thinking to this day: not lie or fiction, as myth is currently understood in American English, but an imaginative attempt to connect complex bodies of data to form a sense of meaning. *Dynamics of Faith*, and specifically the chapter on symbol and myth in theology, forever made it impossible for me to think of theological language as

30   BELIEVING AND ITS TENSIONS

anything but symbolic and mythical. It also alerted
me to the evils that theological literalism can cause.
The few pages of Tillich's that I teach constantly
affect my entire view of how to "do" theology.

> Monotheism also falls under the criticism
> of the myth. It needs, as one says today,
> "demythologization." The word has been
> used in connection with the elaboration
> of the mythical elements in stories and
> symbols of the Bible, both of the Old and
> the New Testaments—stories like those of
> the Paradise, of the fall of Adam, of the
> great flood, of the Exodus from Egypt, of
> the virgin birth of the Messiah, of many
> of his miracles, of his resurrection and
> ascension, of his expected return as the
> judge of the universe.[3]

At The Jewish Theological Seminary, Heschel, a conservative Jew, and Kaplan, a Reconstructionist Jew,
were seen as polar opposites. I never believed that
easy characterizations like heretic and traditionalist
were accurate. I studied with both of them for a few
years, and each contributed mightily to my theological evolution. It was Kaplan above all who moved me
from supernaturalism to a naturalist understanding
of Judaism and of religion in general. Kaplan was the
first serious Jewish thinker to have read widely in the
social sciences, and he understood that if religion

doesn't emerge from a supernatural God, then the only alternative is that it must emerge from the workings of a human community. If that is true of all religions, then it is true of Judaism, too. His entire career was devoted to systematically exposing, reformulating, or (as he would call it later) reconstructing Judaism as a system of naturalist theology. It was Kaplan who first pointed out, in a very powerful moment for me in his classroom, that God did not speak at Sinai, and that therefore—in a claim that rocked me then but that I have repeated so many times since then—Judaism is whatever the Jewish people say it is.

Heschel, of course, did not share Kaplan's naturalist assumptions, but it was Heschel who, more than any other thinker, forced me to think about the nature of God. Yochanan Muffs's notion of the personhood of God stems ultimately from Heschel (who was our common teacher), specifically from the central chapters of his book *The Prophets*, where he suggested that we have to understand the prophetic God as a God of pathos. By *pathos*, Heschel meant

> *If God can hurt us, that means that this God that we understand and experience is a vulnerable God who can be hurt as well.*

feeling. God is not indifferent to the world but cares deeply on many levels about the world, nature, the human community in general, and the Jewish community specifically.

This feeling, emotional God, struck Muffs, and later me, as a powerfully humanizing God. Human beings care. Human beings feel, and that is how God is portrayed in the Bible. Heschel used to say that God is a failure. God never gets what God wants to get. God is constantly frustrated, yet God returns again and again to try to direct human history and the lives of human communities toward certain values that are God-inspired. This notion of a caring God led me to the next step, which I understood to be God's vulnerability. People that we care about have the capacity to hurt us. If God can hurt us, that means that this God that we understand and experience is a vulnerable God who can *be* hurt as well. God's vulnerability is in our hands. This idea helped me expand my understanding of God and is a cornerstone of the complex set of word pictures with which I characterize God.

IMAGES
OF GOD

I find it fascinating that in popular religious thinking, God is portrayed as power. The images are sovereignty, kingship, and judgment. The notion of a vulnerable God—a God who can be hurt, whom we have the power to hurt, and who has a complex emotional life—is commonly ignored.

I frequently use the following midrash as an example: When the Temple was destroyed and Jerusalem burned, the Rabbis portray God as sitting and weeping over the fate of God's people. When the angels come to God and say, "You must not cry— you are God," God's response is, "Woe unto a father who succeeded in his youth and failed in his old age." The Temple was destroyed, Jerusalem had burned down, and the Jewish people were exiled; that this was a failure on God's part is a notion we frequently ignore. The angel again insists that God must not cry. God replies, "If you don't let me cry, I'm going to go into my private bedroom, close the door, lock it, and cry by myself" (Midrash Lamentations Rabbah, proem 24).

In popular religious thinking, God is portrayed as power.

If we add this word picture to what we commonly use as an image of God, we end up with a very different concept of the nature of God. But of course this too is a provisional, tentative image. It doesn't work, or it shouldn't work, on the High Holy Days, for example, when it is important that we think of God as sitting on the throne of judgment and forcing us to account for the lives we have led. There's hardly any sense in the liturgy of the High Holy Days that our sins are an indication of God's failure. But that is also part of the treasury of word pictures that our tradition portrays.

Most of my recent thinking has dealt with specific images of God that I have come across in contemporary Jewish writings on theology. I would like to consider some of these developments, which deal not with broad issues of method but rather with specific images. Here I would like to draw from process theology as well as specifically cite Professor Benjamin Sommer, whose book on the "bodies of God" has had a great effect on me; and Judith Plaskow, a Jewish feminist theologian.

GOD AS A PROCESS

Process theology should no longer be understood as something revolutionary. Mordecai Kaplan was, if anything, a process theologian. Kaplan insisted that God is not a being—not even a nonphysical being—but is rather a power or an impulse. He called it the "power that makes for salvation"—*salvation* being Kaplan's term for fulfillment. The natural order is all there is, of course, for Kaplan, but within this natural order there is a power, an impulse, or a process whose purpose it is to actualize all of our values so they are embodied and can affect everything we do and experience. In one formulation of this idea, Kaplan likened this power to magnetism, which is itself invisible but whose effects can be seen: if you put iron filings on a piece of paper and apply a magnet under the piece of paper, the filings will immediately fall into a certain order, according to the magnetic waves. That's how God functions: we don't see God, but we see the effects of this power that makes for salvation in our actions, in love, in ethical behavior, in the search for sci-

> *Process theology should no longer be understood as something revolutionary. Mordecai Kaplan was, if anything, a process theologian.*

entific truth, and in artistic creativity. So God is not a being; God is not a noun, God is a power, a process, or an impulse; God is a verb, according to Kaplan.

Kaplan's idea of God as a power that makes for salvation caused an uproar among his students. The common question was, How does one pray to a power? Or what does one do with all the other powers in the world that seem to work against the drive for salvation? What to do about the drive toward cruelty, to suffering of all kinds? These are questions that Kaplan deals with, adequately or not, in his writings. But he never abandoned the notion that God is a power, an impulse, or a process, not a being.

GOD AS EMBODIED

The notion that God has a body would seem at first blush to be an even more radical extension of our provisional word pictures of God than Kaplan's idea of God as a process. If there has been any constant in our history of thinking about God, it has been that God is incorporeal. It has always been an assumption that human beings are embodied but that God is not. The thinking that inspired Benjamin Sommer's book *The Bodies of God and the World of Ancient Israel* stems directly from Heschel and Muffs: from Heschel's notion of the divine pathos, that God has a rich emotional life, and from Muffs's notion that the ensemble of word pictures or metaphors for God throughout Jewish literature suggests that God is very much a person—and a person has a body. Sommers acknowledges his debt to Muffs and to Heschel, although he concedes that neither of them suggested that God has a body. Sommers has read the Bible very carefully, and the word pictures for God throughout it suggest, to him, that it is not out-landish to conceive of God as embodied.

GOD AS GENDERLESS

Of these three contemporary revisions in the clas-sic Jewish word pictures of God, feminism is prob-ably the oldest. It dates back to the 1960s as part of the struggle to give Jewish women an equal role in Jewish communal life, in the synagogue and Jewish ritual, and in Jewish theology. The process began with a very powerful protest against the tendency throughout our classical texts and in our popular language to refer to God as a male. God is clearly referred to as *He*, and when we talk about what Jews do, we talk largely about what Jewish *men* do. Women were relegated to sitting behind a partition in the synagogue and were isolated from organized Jewish thinking, Jewish theology, and Jewish institutional life.

Theologically, the most articulate statement of the need to revise God language in Judaism to include women was suggested by Dr. Judith Plaskow in her book *Standing Again at Sinai*. Plaskow devotes an entire chapter to Jewish theological language and the need to stop referring to God as *He* and *Him*; rather, she suggests, either use gender-neutral language altogether or simply alternate *She* and *Her* with *He* and *Him*. Liturgically, this has had a significant effect on the more liberal branches of the Jewish community, including in the Reform and Conservative prayer books. Reconstructionist prayer books no longer refer to God with masculine pronouns.

What is much harder to accomplish, of course, is for this new way of speaking about God to affect our theological thinking and our everyday language. If we now understand that all references to God are word pictures, metaphors crafted by human communities, then why not refer to, or use a series of word pictures that view, God as female?

We're not used to it because we are dealing with a tradition that's three or four thousand years old, when this was unheard of among Jews, and we have to understand that this tradition was composed largely by men. If the images of God in traditional texts stemmed from the authors looking at themselves in the mirror, in effect, then it is quite understandable that what emerged was a God who was a He, who was considered male, who had masculine characteristics, and who was viewed as a father, a king, and so forth.

METHODOLOGICAL ISSUES

In conclusion, there are two methodological issues that must be dealt with. First, given the richness of the divine images that have been collected throughout biblical, rabbinic, midrashic, homiletical, philosophical, and mystical literature, is there any way we can determine whether some are authentic and legitimate, whereas others are questionable?

It's clear that because we do not have a pope or a worldwide chief rabbi, there is no easy way to make these decisions. My sense it that because these images emerged from the experience of the Jewish community, it is precisely only the committed Jewish community that has the right to determine which images of God are helpful or useful, which may be taught, which should be incorporated into the liturgy, and which can be formulated into a theological statement.

For example, within the past few decades, there have been two significant attempts to deal with the problem of evil. How does God handle, accept, or maybe even cause evil and suffering for righteous human beings? One of these answers emerged from the Holocaust. Rabbi Richard Rubenstein proposed that the only theological approach possible after the Holocaust was to identify with the death-of-God theology. "God is dead" became a common theme in American society in the1960s. Rubenstein insists that by claiming that God is dead, we are not actually saying anything about God, because how would *we* know that God is dead? Rather, we are claiming that what has died is the classic Jewish myth: the notion that God cares for the Jewish people. We are left with a cold and unfeeling universe with nothing to support us but our own efforts. What else can a Jew say after Auschwitz?

What is significant here is that Rubenstein promotes a very radical image of God after the Holocaust. It is an image, a metaphor, or a word picture that is familiar to Christians, whose son of God did die and redeem the world of its sins. But a dying God was never an image with which Jews felt comfortable. In fact, it was clearly one of the reasons Judaism and Christianity split two thousand years ago. The metaphor that God has died was never fully accepted by the Jewish people as a whole. It went nowhere, because the community just did not accept it as a legitimate image of God.

The second attempt to deal with the problem of evil came from Rabbi Harold Kushner, whose son died at a very young age from progeria (a rapid-aging disease). Kushner wrote a book, *When Bad Things Happen to Good People*, that had an enormous readership in the Jewish world and internationally; it was translated into many languages. Its theological core is Kushner's claim that God is simply not all-powerful. We are living, he said, with a limited God. God very much wishes to help people recover from suffering, to banish suffering, and to banish diseases of all kind, but God simply cannot do this. Instead, God weeps with us, and while weeping with us, God becomes allied with our own suffering and pain.

In contrast to Rubenstein's notion of the death of God, Kushner's notion of a limited God—of a God who just does not have the power to solve the problem of suffering and the problem of evil—has had a wide appeal and has helped many people, Jewish and non-Jewish, deal with their own suffering. This new image of God has won widespread identification among the Jewish people. Rubenstein's death of God simply did not. Who decided? The community did. Part of the theologically caring community decided, based on how these two new theological images enabled them to deal with their life experiences.

The second methodological issue is the following: What lies beyond the metaphor? If all that we have in recognizing, speaking of, and experiencing God is a wide-ranging treasury of humanly crafted metaphors, images, and word pictures, what, then, is the ultimate reality—if there is one—beyond these pictures? What do they represent? What do they capture? What is the ultimate nature of God? The images are subjective, provisional, scattered, and contradictory. Is that all there is?

I have struggled with this issue for years, and I have come to the conclusion that we probably cannot go beyond the images. In a sense, these images do reflect a higher reality, but that higher reality, the ultimate reality, cannot be captured by the human mind or the human experience. If anything lies beyond the metaphors, it is simply more metaphors—more satisfactory, but equally humanly crafted, images of God, who is ultimately beyond.

This is the God the mystics tried to encounter. If we finally break through, reach, and experience this God, all we could probably do, as Heschel might have said, is sing and dance. What lies beyond our own minds and our

> *What lies beyond the metaphor ... beyond these pictures? What do they represent? What do they capture?*

own experience are insights far beyond the human. We may strive to reach those insights, but they will continue to elude us. How do we know that they are there, then? How do we know that there is a God beyond the images? That constitutes our leap of faith. At the point that we go beyond our minds and our experience and throw ourselves into the ultimately unknown, we *believe*.

CHAPTER 2

Torah

It was my practice to begin teaching Jewish theology with either a unit or at least a chapter on revelation, because revelation had established the issue of authority in all areas of Jewish thought and practice. Whatever authority tradition had, it stemmed from how we understood that tradition's origin. If Jewish tradition had been revealed explicitly by an all-powerful, omniscient divine being, then the authority of the tradition was airtight. It would be mandatory for all Jews to accept these teachings as the will of a supernatural God. If, in contrast, the content of this tradition was shaped in various ways by the human community, then the authority of tradition was invariably weakened, because the human contribution to the formulation of tradition constantly shifted and changed as the Jewish community moved through history.

The extent, then, to which the Jewish past in matters of belief and practice is binding on the contemporary community is the result of the extent to which God's will and God's word were behind traditional Jewish teaching. The more extensive God's role, the more powerful the authority. The less extensive God's role and the more extensive the human contribution to the shaping of revelation, the less authoritative the past would be; the community of each generation would then have the opportunity and the responsibility to review the content of tradition and evaluate it in terms of the insights, needs, and understanding of that community.

In this book, I decided to abandon the approach of beginning with revelation, and instead begin with the issue of God. It occurred to me that there was not much point in trying to discuss revelation independently of how I understand God. Indeed, as I was teaching revelation, I often used to consider that I was saying just as much about how I understood God as I was teaching revelation. For example, if I believe that "God speaks" is a literal truth, then I have a literal understanding of revelation and the words of chapters 19 and 20 in Exodus were God's explicit words—and God revealed the the Torah verbally in words and letters to our ancestors.

And God spoke these words, saying: I the LORD am your God who brought you out of the land of Egypt, the house of bondage: You shall have no other gods besides Me. You shall not make for yourself a sculptured image, or any likeness of what is in the heavens above, or on the earth below, or in the waters under the earth. You shall not bow down to them or serve them. For I the LORD your God am an impassioned God, visiting the guilt of the parents upon the children, upon the third and the fourth generation of those who reject Me, but showing kindness to the thousandth generation of those who love Me and keep My commandments.

(EXODUS 20:1–6)

As soon as I began to teach revelation, then, I was beginning to teach about God. I did not understand the Torah's statements about God, God's nature, and God's activity as literally true. *Speaking*, when applied to God, would be just one of many metaphors used to describe God in our classical literature. That is why I began this book with God—everything I understand about God and the language used to describe God. Now I am prepared to discuss a specific activity attributed to God by our tradition: revelation.

REVELATION VERSUS
INSTRUCTION

I now question the English word that I used in all of my previous teachings and writings. *Revelation* sounds strange to Jewish ears. My late teacher Professor Max Kadushin used to say that if there's no Hebrew word for something, then it is not Jewish; it doesn't belong in Judaism. There really is no specific Hebrew term for the English word *revelation*. The term is, however, everywhere in Christian theology, because the core component of that faith is that God was revealed in human form as Jesus of Nazareth to a community of Jews in the first century of the common era. A literal episode and experience of revelation is therefore at the root of Christianity. But there is no parallel root experience of God's self-revelation in Jewish sources. Indeed, throughout the Torah, we are told repeatedly that no human being can see God. Even Moses was told that "no human being can see Me and live" (Exodus 33:20). In the most striking account of Moses's request to see God, God instructs Moses to stand in the cleft of a rock; God then passes by Moses, but Moses sees only the back of God.

> And the LORD said, "See, there is a place
> by Me. Station yourself on the rock and,
> as my Presence passes by, I will put you in
> a cleft of the rock and shield you with My

hand until I have passed by. Then I will
take My hand away and you will see My
back; but My face shall not be seen."

(EXODUS 33:21–23)

If "no human being can see Me and live" is the case
with Moses, then how much more so would it be for
any of the other human beings who populate our
Torah. There are references to Isaiah's seeing God
in chapter 7 of that book, and Ezekiel in his mystical vision of the Chariot sees something that he
describes in very elusive terms as God, but these are
very rare. Nobody else—not even Abraham, Isaac, or
Jacob—literally sees God.

What, then, can Jews understand by the term *revelation*? It is not unusual for us to adopt that term
when we discuss theology with other faith communities, because it does capture the significant issue of
God's authoritative disclosure of God's will and of
God's being. But for the title of this chapter, I have
reverted to the much more traditional term *Torah*,
the Hebrew word for "instruction." When we speak
of the origin of the Jewish religion and God's role in
that, we imply something very different from God's
self-revelation. The origin of our tradition lies in God
teaching something about everything: the nature of
God, God's will, God's plans for the Jewish people,
God's concern, God's feelings—all of these in a sense
are *revealed*, but they are, in Jewish terms, much more
explicitly *taught*. Hence the term *Torah*.

Upon further reflection, however, the move from the term *revelation* to the term *instruction* is much more than a verbal issue. Revelation requires an active God. What is hidden, God now determines to reveal, and the audience for this revelation must have a stance of acceptance. God reveals to Israel; God is acting and Israel is passive. It's true that Israel's appropriation of that revelation is itself an activity. That's why instruction is, by its very nature, an interactive experience. The teacher and the student become involved together in developing the content of the material that is being discussed. In the evolution of Jewish tradition, teaching was in fact the central mode of transmission, and teaching in every aspect of Judaism became very interactive.

For example, just look at a page of Talmud. Nothing there goes unchallenged. Everything is suggested, picked up, sometimes refuted, sometimes accepted, and sometimes reformulated, and even the teacher is more of a participant in the process than one who dictates the truth. This is extraordinarily suggestive of how the tradition was transmitted from generation to generation and from God to the community itself. God's teaching demanded a response, and Israel's legitimate task was to respond. If the central mode of the transmission of the tradition was an interactive experience, then why not the original formulation of the experience itself?

VARIOUS VIEWS OF
REVELATION

In *Sacred Fragments*, I reviewed a series of options on how to understand what I then called revelation. These options ranged from a strong traditionalist position, in which God is portrayed as having revealed the Torah in discrete words and letters, to, at the other end of the spectrum, a naturalist or humanist position in which humanity shapes its conception of God's revelation in light of human predilections. In place of *revelation*, naturalists use the term *discovery*. In this most liberal stance, normally attributed to Mordecai Kaplan, Israel discovers the Torah. "God reveals" is only a different way of saying "Israel discovers." Discovering is, of course, a human activity. For Kaplan, the classical humanist, Torah and revelation demand the human initiative. I wrote:

> We have come full circle. We opened our discussion of revelation by noting that our three subissues—the principle, the fact, and the content—of revelation were inextricably intertwined, that the way we dealt with any of the three issues would inevitably predetermine how we would deal with the other two. Our review of the various attempts to define the content of revelation indicates that at

least for three of our thinkers—Kaplan,
Rosenzweig, and Heschel—the only way
of approaching all of these questions
is to reject the literalness of the biblical account of revelation and to posit
that no human characterization of God
and His activity can be understood as
objectively true. Rather, all such characterizations have to be understood as
metaphorical attempts to capture what
is inherently beyond the range of human
experience.[4]

There are a number of different versions of a position in which both God and the human community participate in shaping the content of revelation. These different versions have been advocated
by theologians such as Abraham Joshua Heschel,
Martin Buber, and Franz Rosenzweig. For Heschel,
we do not have what God revealed in its purity.
What we have is an interpretation, a midrash, of
God's content. God did reveal a content, but only
God knows that content. We have a human version
of it. God's revealed Torah must pass through the
scrim of human understanding and human language. What emerges, then, is a human version of
God's revelation.

Buber and Rosenzweig, both classical existential-
ists, advocate that what God revealed was essentially
God's self, in an active relationship with Israel. God

did not reveal a content; God simply revealed. God entered a relationship with the Jewish people. The Torah, then, is the human response to—not the record of—God's self-revelation to the human community. It spells out what it means to have been a participant in this revelatory moment and how that should affect the ongoing relationship of God and the community.

Both of these positions I understood to be intermediate steps, stages between the traditionalist God's revelation in discrete words and letters and Kaplan's revelation as human discovery. Heschel, Buber, and Rosenzweig postulate that both partners in the relationship are active. God reveals, but the human role in understanding or appropriating that revelation makes the people a participant in the exchange.

In my initial presentation of these options in *Sacred Fragments*, I settled much more comfortably in advocating for these middle-of-the-road positions—probably coming closer to Heschel's notion that God revealed a sacred content that had to be transmitted through the scrim of the human mind and human language so that it became a human document at the end.

> Decisions between theological options should never be made on the basis of one issue alone, even as central an issue as revelation. It may yet be helpful,

in a preliminary way, to suggest how
various criteria figure in reaching such
decisions....

We have appealed to four such criteria: theological coherence, historical
authenticity, programmatic implications, and psychological inadequacy.
First, is the position theologically coherent on its own terms? Second, does it
have an authentically Jewish ring? Third,
what are its implications for the decisions that face the Jewish community
today? Finally, does the position meet
the psychological needs of the individual
believer?[5]

I suggested then that the distinctions among Heschel,
Kaplan, Buber, and Rosenzweig are not that great.
Once you allow a human contribution to the content of Jewish tradition, you have assigned a degree of
relativity that is totally absent from the traditionalist
position.

The significant gap then lies between all of these
views and the traditionalist option, in which God
reveals every word of Torah, making the authority
of the Torah binding on all Jews everywhere forever. In this view, God's will is simply not open to
cultural changes. In contrast, once you admit that
the human community had some contributory role
in the formulation of what it was that God willed,

then you have substantially weakened the sense of absolute authority and have opened the Torah to being considered as a cultural document that reflects the will of the community, or at least the community's understanding of God's will. That, of course, is subject to change, development, and a pluralistic understanding of God's will.

THE MEANING OF "GOD REVEALS"

I am now inclined to believe that the various versions of this liberal position are inadequate. Reflecting on some of my conclusions in chapter 1, I must ask what it means to say that God reveals anything. How can we understand God's role in revelation in any conceivable way? If God is active in the revelatory moment, that role is itself captured in human language. "God reveals" is itself a human version of some divine activity that we cannot capture literally. We are back, then, in the position of characterizing the entire experience as a matter of faith. I increasingly believe that when we say that God revealed the Torah we mean that this is the human attempt to understand God's will through the act of human discovery, assigning the most active role possible to the human community. It seems to me that if we have replaced the term *revelation* with the term *Torah*, we have in fact characterized the human encounter with the divine—in the world, in nature, in history, and in all the varieties of human experience—as an exchange.

That brings me back to the classroom. When revelation is viewed in this way, what happens in the classroom may be a replica of the revelation we study in the Torah. In the classroom, the teacher may present material, but the students are active participants in grappling with the material. Scientists who try to understand the makeup of the world can discover and try to formulate what lies beyond the human community. One of my colleagues, the microbiologist Robert Pollack, once said in a lecture at Columbia University that God has revealed two texts: the Torah and nature. My sense now is that the Torah is much more like nature in terms of the roles of God and humanity in appropriating and understanding what lies beyond us.

> *When revelation is viewed in this way, what happens in the classroom may be a replica of the revelation we study in the Torah.*

Most attempts to wrest a theology of revelation out of the Bible focus on chapters 19 and 20 of the book of Exodus, the Sinai revelation. Benjamin Sommer, who teaches at The Jewish Theological

Seminary, has revisited the Sinai revelation by comparing it to other revelatory accounts in the Bible—specifically in the books of Exodus and Deuteronomy, but also, in an extraordinary exegetical leap, in the book of 1 Kings. This intertextual approach reveals an understanding of the biblical account of revelation that demonstrates possibly pluralistic understandings of what really happened at Sinai and provides biblical support for some of the liberal positions that have been adopted by contemporary Jewish theologians.[6]

WHAT HAPPENED AT SINAI?

Sommer asks whether the Exodus 19 Sinai account was visual, auditory, or both. If it were auditory, what was heard: words, thunder, or other sounds? Chronologically, where does the Sinai revelation fit in with the later references to the Sinai story in the book of Exodus? Finally, how does the Deuteronomy 5 account expand, enlighten, or clarify what took place at Sinai? All of these questions are explored in great detail by Professor Sommer through close examination of the biblical texts themselves and of later classical Jewish commentaries.

But it is the 1 Kings version that is most interesting to modern liberal theologians, for in chapter 19, the prophet Elijah experiences a revelation from God in which God is not in thunder, wind, or fire;

God is no place in the visual or auditory aspects of the revelation. Rather, God appears to Elijah in what the Bible calls *kol d'mamah dakah*:

> "Come out," He called, "and stand on the mountain before the LORD." And lo, the LORD passed by. There was a great and mighty wind, splitting mountains and shattering rocks by the power of the LORD; but the LORD was not in the wind. After the wind—an earthquake; but the LORD was not in the earthquake. After the earthquake—a fire, but the LORD was not in the fire. And after the fire—a soft murmuring sound.
>
> (1 KINGS 19:11–12)

Those final three words—*kol d'mamah dakah*—have been variously interpreted by biblical scholars, but we can make a case for saying that the term means the "voice [or sound] of silence." The classical translation is "a still small voice," but a still small voice at the extreme is silence. That God appears in the silence itself is very familiar to those of us today who understand that silence can be very loud.

So if the Israelite community at Sinai didn't see anything, didn't hear words, or didn't want to hear anything but delegated Moses to do the exchanges with God—or if there was nothing to hear apart from the silence—this suggests that

God's revelation was very much as it is described by contemporary liberal theologians: that what God revealed at Sinai was God's self. The Buber and Rosenzweig position suggests that what God revealed was God in relationship, with no content. But in Sommer's account, content is restored in the form of a pregnant silence: God's presence revealed to the community.

Sommer quotes a very famous passage from a Hasidic master, Rabbi Mendl of Rimanov (recorded by Gershom Scholem, the master scholar of mysticism and Hasidism), that all that was revealed at Sinai was the aleph of the first word of the Ten Commandments, *anochi*. Aleph, of course, is the first letter of the Hebrew alphabet. By itself it has no sound; it is a silent letter. It becomes vocalized when a vowel of some kind is added to it, but in the Torah there are no vowels, so the silent aleph stands for itself. Rabbi Mendl suggested that that contains all of revelation.

The suggestion, then, is that almost any specific content to the revelational experience would be limiting to God's power and to God's will. For God's revelation of the Torah to be maximalist—to mean as much as it can possibly mean while also meaning whatever the receiver of the revelation hears—it must, in fact, be silence. Composers understand very well that the silence between notes or chords is itself part of the musical content. Silence is the most extensive possible content of any exchange.

MYTH AS AN
ORGANIZING POWER

I return now to the conceptualizations that characterize my theological thinking: my serious attempts to avoid all literalism in my characterization of God and my use of the term *myth* as the organizing power that shapes the content of Jewish theology. Myths as I have characterized them are created by a community that hears. If we accept the fact that all experience, seeing, and hearing (specifically, in this case) require interpretation by the human partner in the exchange, then we are saying that the human contribution to the experience is what shapes it, gives it form, and gives it meaning. Neurologically, this corresponds to the work of the brain, which is active in all of our senses. We do not experience the world as a blank slate. We experience the world filled with meaning; that is our legitimate interpretive role, and at least part of that role is shaped by the brain. A myth, as I understand it, is precisely the shaping factor that takes chaotic and confusing data and gives it a specific order. Turning chaos into order may be as much a cognitive necessity as a theological act. This, you will recall, is what the anthropologist Clifford Geertz suggested is the role of religion. Religion is an ordering device, and myth is one of the ways in which this ordering takes place.

In terms of Professor Sommer's use of 1 Kings 19 and Elijah, it is very possible to read that event as God's revelation through a still small voice or, as I would prefer, as the sound of silence. If what God revealed was the sound of silence, what Elijah heard was shaped by his total understanding of who the God of Israel is, what this God wishes, and what meaning God has in God's encounter with the prophet Elijah. Finally, if we read this sound of silence back to the Sinai account and understand it that way, then at Sinai the Israelites saw no portraits or pictures, nor did they hear any sounds. As Mendl of Rimanov suggests, what they heard was the silent aleph, which itself was soundless but which is the source of all possible meaning, and they emerged from that experience with what we today call the Torah.

I return now to the issue of authority. The various contemporary positions on revelation that I outlined earlier in this chapter span the range of possibilities from a literalist (i.e., a verbal revelation) view, to the more moderate attempts to affect God's revelatory content (which may not be verbal), to a more liberal position, in which God either appears or is revealed in loving relationship (or, per Rosenzweig, a loving and commanding relationship), to Kaplan's position that revelation is actually a human discovery. My view is now closest to Kaplan's echoing of Elijah's sound of silence and Sommer's interpretation of the Sinai episode, in which the active partner in all accounts of divine revelation is the human being, the receiver of the revelation. What God reveals, what emerges from God, we don't know. But we do know what the human community understood as God's will for it. This community transformed it, recorded it, and characterized it for the future life of the community. This means, of course, that there was no specified content to the revelation, that even back at Sinai it was the human community that determined what was revealed and that gave it shape, content, and meaning. What resulted was a pluralistic, subjective, evolutionary understanding of the Torah. Nothing is fixed, literal, or objectively true, but everything is tentative, provisional, and endlessly open to human reinterpretation.

THE CENTRALITY OF LAW
IN JUDAISM

In theology, this reality makes a minimal difference. It is the unfortunate experience of the Jewish theologian to realize that throughout classical Judaism, it was halacha (the Law) not Aggadah (the lore) that was subject to rigorous codification. Think of how much literature has been devoted to shaping and codifying Jewish law to this day. In contrast, there are relatively few Jewish scholars who have worked on issues of theology, what Jews are supposed to believe. Therefore, if we reconsider the role of authority and shape it according to our understanding of revelation, then the area that will be most strikingly affected will be Jewish law rather than Jewish theology. And halacha is of particular concern to contemporary Jewish communities. The major differences between these communities most clearly involve their interpretations of such issues as feminism, homosexuality, liturgical change, and ritual observance of the Sabbath and Jewish holidays. The range from ultra-Orthodoxy to liberal Reform can be understood in terms of what each community decides to abandon and retain, who makes that decision, and most significantly, the theological assumptions that underlie each of these approaches. And the theology is based on how we understand revelation. Is it discrete words and letters, is it a matter of content that has to be interpreted by the community, is it God's self, or is it the silent aleph?

How and why did law achieve such a central role in the classic Jewish myth? That should not be taken for granted. Christianity has explicitly disparaged the centrality of law and replaced it with the centrality of faith or belief. Believe in Jesus and you will be saved, Christians are taught. The origin of Christianity as an independent faith community was determined when Paul insisted in his Epistle to the Romans that a human community can have an independent passageway to God without observing Jewish law. Until then, Christianity was a subset of Judaism; you had to become a Jew if you were to become a Christian. Now Christianity is an independent faith community. Men, for example, do not have to be circumcised to become Christians. But for Jews, from the very beginning—from biblical law through the development of rabbinic law in the Mishnah, the Talmud, the Code of Jewish Law, and the responsa literature—Jewish law has defined the Jewish religious experience.

If we believe that the Torah was revealed literally and explicitly by God, then law has had such a central role in Judaism because that's what God wanted, so that's what Judaism undertook. But if we reject this understanding of revelation and believe that Judaism was shaped by the Jewish community, then a different kind of answer is necessary.

> *Law is, by nature, a conservative force. The liberal impulse has to struggle against conservative tendencies to retain the law as it has always been....*

There are various approaches to this, none of which are entirely convincing. One is that law was central to all of the other communities that surrounded the Israelites in biblical times. For instance, the Code of Hammurabi, the Babylonian law code, contains much that found its way into the Torah—though frequently amended, revised, and sometimes completely changed. The Israelites may have simply adopted a common form of religious expression among the neighboring communities.

A second possibility is that if we take Clifford Geertz's suggestion seriously that religion is an ordering device, then law becomes central to its task of ordering: ordering human behavior, communal behavior, human relationships, and even the community's relationship to God.

My sense, however, is that the power of law in Judaism stems not from its theology but from more internal sources. Namely, it is individual humans who very much need help in providing some order to their behavior and their relationships. Law is, by nature, a conservative force. The liberal impulse has to struggle against conservative tendencies to retain the law as it has always been, and sometimes it takes a very powerful external source, such as sociology or anthropology, to counter the psychological pull of the conservative tendency to retain the law. Whatever the reason, the classical Jewish myth featured law as a symbol and gave it a primary role in the ordering work of religion.

CHAPTER 3

Suffering

I walked through the halls of the Memorial Sloan-Kettering Cancer Center and passed a fourteen-year-old boy sitting in a wheelchair, attached to an IV drip, wearing a baseball cap, and obviously having no hair. I knew what this little boy was suffering from.

Just a few doors from my office at The Jewish Theological Seminary is the office of a colleague, a professor in another department, who is now retired but who for many years was a respected member of our faculty. One day last summer, we were waiting for the elevator, and I noticed that he was wearing a short-sleeved shirt. On his arm was a tattooed number, a reminder of his childhood experience in Auschwitz.

I often tune into an all-news station here in New York, and one day I heard the following: Apparently a tree had fallen along the highway leading into New York. It was a beautiful day: no wind, no rain, just a falling tree—which, as it fell, hit a car. In that car was a family: in the front seat, a father, who was driving, and his wife, a mother, sitting next to him; in the backseat, an infant strapped into a car seat. The tree fell over the front of the car, immediately killing the father and the mother. The child in the backseat was unharmed.

These are but three of the kinds of experiences that many of us have to undergo at just about any time in our lives.

Most frequently, the issue that these scenarios raise is called the "problem of evil." That's what I read in most books of theology, including my own, *Sacred Fragments:*

> The focus of all theological speculation about the place of evil in the world is its relationship to God. The dilemma is clear: If God is omnipotent, then He is in some way responsible for evil. If He is not responsible, then He is not omnipotent; then evil exists independently of God's will and God's sovereignty is severely impaired. The choice lies between an omnipotent God who is responsible for evil and a limited God who is not.[7]

I prefer to call it the "problem of suffering," however, because suffering is what happens when we experience the evil that comes from outside us. I refer here not to the evil that we instigate ourselves—that's another problem—but to the evil that comes to us from other human beings, from nature, or from an unknown source. As a theological question, this experience of human suffering—particularly when it seems to be unjustified, random, and extraordinarily painful, both physically and emotionally—is the greatest challenge to our faith commitment, to our relationship to God, or, to use anthropologist Clifford Geertz's formulation, to our sense that the world is fundamentally ordered.

> *As a theological question, this experience of human suffering is the greatest challenge to our faith commitment, to our relationship to God.*

These three incidents seem to us to be expressions of chaos. And if Geertz is correct that the task of religion is to discipline the chaos in the world and order our experience of the universe, then this human suffering above all challenges what religion is all about. The technical theological term for the enterprise of trying to account for the chaotic elements in our experience is *theodicy*, which comes from two Greek words, *theos* (God) and *dike* (to justify or vindicate). Theodicy, then, is the attempt to make God straight again, to vindicate and to reaffirm God's justice in the world, despite what happens to us, despite our sense that even as the world seems to be ordered from some perspectives, from other perspectives it seems to be eminently chaotic.

THE CHALLENGE OF CHAOS

Geertz himself, toward the end of the seminal article that I have been quoting earlier in this book, suggests that the attack on the sense of an ordered world posed by the apparent emergence of the chaotic can be further analyzed and reduced to three specific challenges: the intellectual, the emotional, and the moral.

The intellectual challenge is simply the attempt to understand from where this experience of chaos emerged, how and why this totally unexpected and tragic event took place. For example, after a major airplane crash in which hundreds of people are killed, we spend millions trying to understand what happened to the airplane that made it crash. The challenge is simply to understand. It is an intellectual challenge because it assumes that part of our sense of the chaotic is simply the randomness of the entire experience. That's why we sometimes need to do an autopsy after a sudden unexpected death. Although the autopsy does not return the person to life, it helps us deal with his or her death because it helps us understand why that death happened.

The emotional challenge is simply, how to mourn. How do we suffer? How do we live with the pain? How do we accumulate the resources within ourselves, within our friends, and within our community to enable us to survive the pain and not give up?

If God is not fair, then why do we need God in the first place? Furthermore, if God is not fair, then why should we be fair?

The moral challenge is the most familiar to us. It is based on the notion that God is supposed to treat us morally and ethically. The death, calamity, or other form of chaos is just not fair. If it's not fair, then God is not fair. And if God is not fair, then why do we need God in the first place? Furthermore, if God is not fair, then why should we be fair?

There are two classic Jewish responses to the challenge of chaos: the enigma response and the punishment response. The enigma response is basically not a response at all; it's a surrender. The enigma response says there *is* no response—live with it. We don't understand our suffering and we don't even try to understand it; instead, we live with it and bear it as well as we can, and we don't subject God to moral judgments. God is God, doing whatever God does for whatever reasons, and we merely accept it. This is an ancient response to the challenge of suffering. It's in all of the classical texts, and we hear it very frequently today—for example, when we mourn the death of an infant. We don't claim to understand why an infant dies; we simply accept the fact and the need to suffer, and we certainly don't condemn God for the death.

The punishment response is theologically based on the repeated threat throughout scripture that if we accept God's commands, then all blessings will flow to us, but if we rebel and disobey God, then all kinds of punishments will follow, including illness, famine, and military defeat. Consider this paragraph that Jews recite twice daily:

> "If you will earnestly heed the mitzvot that I gave you this day, to love the Lord your God and to serve Him with all your heart and all your soul, then I will favor your land with rain at the proper season—rain in autumn and rain in spring—and you will have an ample harvest of grain and wine and

oil. I will assure abundance in the fields
for your cattle. You will eat to content-
ment. Take care lest you be tempted
to forsake God and turn to false Gods
in worship. For then the wrath of the
Lord your God will be directed against
you. He will close the heavens and hold
back the rain; the earth will not yield its
produce. You will soon disappear from
the good land which the Lord is giving
you."

(DEUTERONOMY 11:13–17)

The punishment response is also omnipresent in
our classical texts, and even to this day, to the
horror of many Jews, it is used in ultra-Orthodox
circles to vindicate God's judgment through the
Holocaust. The Holocaust was God's punishment
for the "sins" of Zionism, of Reform Judaism, of
assimilation, of the creation of the modern state
of Israel—of everything that the ultra-Orthodox
communities disapprove of.

In contrast to the enigma response, the punishment response meets all three challenges of theodicy.
Intellectually, we understand why this suffering has
to take place, because wherever we look we can easily
find sin. Emotionally, we repent and try to change our
lives, because we have the assurance that if we do this,
God's punishment will turn into a blessing. Morally,
we understand that God was justified, because we

were prepared for the fact that when we sin, God will punish us. Thus, God is totally vindicated.

For many of us, neither of these classic responses works. The punishment response assumes that we accept all references in the Torah to God's blessings and curses as literally God's word. It assumes that we know what God wants and that if we don't follow God's word, we must acknowledge the need to be punished. If we reject that entire theological assumption about the nature of the authority of the Torah and its view of the God of Israel, then clearly this literalistic punishment response must be rejected, too.

At least the enigma response doesn't attempt to foist any moral or literally true characteristics upon God. Nevertheless, its very refusal to deal with any of the issues raised by catastrophe leaves us with a sense of incompleteness.

There is another major challenge to the punishment response: the book of Job. Here we have the story of a man who was acknowledged to be righteous, yet who suffered terribly, for reasons we are never told and for reasons Job is never told. God spends six chapters of the book trying to repress Job's questions and never really explains anything. There are, in the end, two ways of explaining and understanding Job's response to God. The conventional response is that Job finally simply accepted God's judgment and withdrew his challenge. The less conventional response—with which I agree—has Job effectively saying to God, "Have it your way!" Job acknowledged that he would never understand why God made him suffer this way.

> *Job said in reply to the LORD:*
> *I know that You can do everything,*
> *That nothing you propose is*
>   *impossible for You.*
> *Who is this who obscures counsel*
>   *without knowledge?*
> *Indeed I spoke without*
>   *understanding,*
> *Of things beyond me, which*
>   *I did not know.*
> *Hear now, and I will speak;*
> *I will ask, and You will*
>   *inform me.*
> *I had heard You with my ears,*
> *But now I see you with my eyes;*
> *Therefore, I recant and relent,*
> *Being but dust and ashes.*
>
> (JOB 42:1–6)

With these two classic responses shown to be basically inadequate, where do we go from here? I would be thrilled if I could suggest that there is an absolutely authoritative and true response to the problems raised by human suffering. If God cannot be held responsible for human suffering then we must turn to human beings as the only alternative.

GOD'S ROLE IN
HUMAN SUFFERING

We cannot speak about God's role in human suffering unless we invoke everything I said in chapter 1
about how we understand God. In other words, we
cannot now revert to a literalist understanding of
God, insisting that the portrayal of God in all of
our classical texts is an accurate picture of the God
who is beyond all human portrayals. Therefore,
when we talk about God's role in human suffering, we have to continue to insist that what we are
talking about is not the God beyond but the God
who is within the metaphors, the word pictures
that we use in understanding our traditional literature and our theological speculations. All that we
have of God as human beings are humanly crafted
word pictures, and all of these word pictures—in
fact, all theological claims—have to be understood
as tentative, provisional, subjective, and pluralistic,
because none is literally true. With that in mind, let
us now pursue our inquiry.

Recall the example I used earlier of Richard
Rubenstein's death-of-God response to the Holocaust.
Rubenstein suggested that the only appropriate
theological response to God's place in the Holocaust
is to proclaim the death of God, thereby associating
himself with the school of Protestant theology in
the midst of the Vietnam War era. But Rubenstein
acknowledged that what he meant was not that God

actually has died, because how can we know that? Rather, what has died is the ensemble of myths, rituals, metaphors, and images that have characterized God's relationship with the world and with the Jewish people since antiquity. The myth died, not God, and the death of the myth simply means that we can no longer invoke everything that we have said about God since Jews began trying to characterize God. We have to move in an entirely different direction and adopt an entirely new set of images, metaphors, and myths to deal with Jewish religious life after the Holocaust.

> *When we talk about God's role in human suffering, we have to continue to insist that what we are talking about is not the God beyond but the God who is within the metaphors.*

As I have already noted, Rubenstein's response was largely dismissed as inauthentic by the Jewish community. But this type of response can be invoked by any individual who has experienced a massive tragedy and who has concluded that he or she can no longer believe that God cares about humanity.

There are two further attempts to deal with the problem of human suffering, one Holocaust-related and the other not. Both echo the concern that led Rubenstein to abandon the entire classical Jewish image of God, but neither is quite as radical as Rubenstein was. What is significant about these two is that they reject much of the conventional classical image of God and attempt to reformulate that image in ways that are strikingly untraditional.

The first is by Rabbi Harold Kushner, whose book *When Bad Things Happen to Good People* was discussed earlier. Rabbi Kushner's son, who had a genetic disease characterized by rapid aging, died when he was fourteen years old with the body of a ninety-year-old. Kushner could not abide the possibility that God was punishing his son or that God in fact had anything to do with the illness that attacked the young boy. Using Mordecai Kaplan's notion of a God who is not omnipotent, Kushner proposes that in fact the only way to deal adequately in theological terms with a God who allowed this terrible genetic disease to attack his son was by positing the notion that God is simply not omnipotent. There is much that God can do, but much that God cannot do, and in this case God must simply stand by, weep with Kushner and his family, and hope that someday, sometime, someone will come up with a cure that will remove the scourge of this illness from the face of creation. What Kushner does then is use the plasticity of the classic word picture of God to reformulate it and to propose a very

unconventional image in its place. Kushner's view is
neither punishment nor enigma. Although Kushner's
book is not primarily a theological treatise, it has
brought a great deal of consolation to many suffering
families around the world.

The other theologian who has worked in the
same general area with different results is Rabbi
Irving (Yitz) Greenberg, an Orthodox rabbi who
is very active and influential within the American
Jewish community and very much not accepted by
some of the Orthodox world because of a variety of
theological claims that he has advanced. Greenberg,
in contrast to Kushner, deals specifically with the
Holocaust, and at various points in his career he has
proposed adjustments that he believes make it possible for us to deal theologically with the Holocaust
experience.

Some decades ago, in a major address at a confer-
ence sponsored by the Episcopalian Cathedral of St.
John the Divine in New York, Greenberg picked up
the implications of the notion of the eclipse of God
that had been advanced decades earlier by Martin
Buber, author of *I and Thou*, which proposes that
our awareness of God comes out of encounters that
are very individual, subjective, and temporary. He
called this the *I-Thou experience*. Buber suggested
that our experience of God is momentary. He spoke
of "moment faith" and "moment God." Greenberg
proposed these formulas as a way of dealing with the
moments when God is in eclipse, when the world

seems to be abandoned, and when faith fails us. It's not a very traditional notion, but it's an understanding of the human relationship with God that can help us deal with massive tragedies such as the Holocaust.

UNDERSTANDING THE HOLOCAUST

In a much later paper, Greenberg proposed that the Holocaust forces us to reformulate what God's covenant with the Jewish people can possibly mean. He proposes that now, with the Holocaust as part of our experience, God's covenant with Israel and Israel's acceptance of that covenant is totally voluntary. Israel can no longer feel bound by the covenant that God made with our ancestors; God no longer has any right to demand obedience to the covenant. However we propose to respond within the covenant framework has to be acceptable to God.

The power in the relationship has shifted. The Jewish people now have the power and the authority. God can no longer command; God simply waits for the Jewish people to respond in whatever way they wish. This theological reformulation of covenant is the basis for Greenberg's highly pluralistic understanding of the American Jewish community, which permits him to include everything from ultra-Orthodox to classical Reform as authentic expressions of Jewish loyalty in the post-Holocaust age.

By far, the iconic response to the Holocaust experience in our day has been provided by Elie Wiesel. Wiesel, a child survivor of Auschwitz, has authored a number of different memoirs, novels, dramas, and poems in an attempt to understand his experience. Of these many responses—not all of them consistent—the one that has had the most widespread impact was his first autobiographical novel, *Night*. *Night* describes Wiesel's experience as a young boy from a small town in Hungary who was imprisoned together with his father. Wiesel's father died in captivity. Wiesel himself was liberated, went to France, and later came to the United States, where he has become a popular lecturer, a novelist, a Nobel Prize winner, an activist on behalf of human rights and Israel, and a professor at Boston University.

One memorable scene in *Night* has provoked reams of commentary. The concentration camp guards accuse three inmates of stealing some soup, erect gallows with three nooses, and command the entire population of the camp to observe the hangings. One of the three who is hanged, a young child, is perceived as struggling. A voice from the crowd of inmates shouts, "Where is God now?," to which a second voice responds, "There is God, hanging on the gallows."

What was Wiesel's intent here? For many interpreters, Wiesel was associating himself with the death-of-God school in theology. For others, Wiesel was saying that God may not be dead yet, but is

surely dying. For still others, Wiesel was portray-
ing a suffering God, a familiar theme from biblical
prophecy.

In a discussion I had with Wiesel when I was
teaching his works at the Skirball Center for Adult
Jewish Learning, I dared to ask him what his intent
was in those pages. He smiled and said that no other
passage in all of his published works had prompted
such an amount of controversy. He insisted that
what he did mean must remain ambiguous, but he
added that it was certainly not his intent to portray
the death of God. "How could I possibly believe
that God was dead?" he asked. "I emerged from the
Holocaust and remained a traditional observant Jew,
largely because of my loyalty to the commitments in
the family in which I was raised and the community
to which I belonged."

SUFFERING AND THE
METAPHOR FOR GOD

As we noted earlier, the notion of a suffering and
dying God is totally familiar to Christians, because
the entire point of Christianity is that the Son
of God died for the sins of humanity. For many
Christians, the account of this death (and subsequent resurrection) is totally literal—not a myth
at all. My rabbinical students who are training for
a hospital chaplaincy frequently find themselves
working together with Christian seminarians, and

the two groups share experiences. My students frequently come back to me bereft. Their Christian colleagues have Jesus's suffering to offer to a suffering patient in a hospital room, whereas, my students tell me, we have nothing to match that. My answer is to suggest that they explore the prophetic and midrashic expressions of God's suffering over the fate of Israel. The God of the Hebrew scriptures may never have been portrayed as dead, but that God is frequently portrayed as being in great pain over the fate of God's chosen people. A suffering humanity is a familiar theme to Jews, from the reading of scripture.

Greenberg and Kushner have made significant adjustments to the classical metaphors for God that have guided our tradition until now. They have used the plasticity attributed to all word pictures to reformulate them and propose alternative understandings of God that enable us to deal with tragedy. Both of these are attempts to deal with the three challenges posed by Clifford Geertz when chaos intrudes upon our attempts to order our experience of the world.

What is important, however, is that both of these responses to suffering involve a major adjustment to the classical Jewish theological myth. They do not deny the viability of the myth in its entirety, as Rubenstein's response does, but both do claim that significant elements have to be revised. Neither claims to say anything at all about the God who lies beyond the myth and the metaphor. Of that, we know nothing.

Earlier in this book I mentioned a conversation I had with a fourth-grade student in a Jewish day school. Ten years ago, at a different school, I was invited to talk about God, this time with a second-grade class. Again, as is my practice, I began by asking the students to talk to me about their own images of God, which they did in some detail. A number of them volunteered to draw images of God on the blackboard, but I noticed that a young girl in the front row had been silent throughout this discussion. So I asked her if she had anything to contribute, and she replied, "Sure—when I think of God, I think about a waterfall."

I said, "Waterfall?" "Yes," she explained. "In our country house in the backyard there is a waterfall, and this helps me think about God because when I sit near the waterfall, I feel refreshed and cool and just good about myself, my family, and the world. And that's what happens when I think about God, too."

I was stunned, but the best was yet to come. Before I could move on with my own agenda, she added, "But then, there are the rocks."

I said to her, "Rocks? What are the rocks?"

She answered, "Before I get to where the waterfall is, I have to walk through a whole field of rocks that are in the way, and I have to make my way all around and through these rocks until I can get to sit next to the waterfall."

I gulped a bit and said, "So what are the rocks like?"

She said, "The rocks are like all the other things that stand in the way of my coming to be close to God."

"Such as?" I prompted. And this second-grader listed racial prejudice, poverty, warfare, disease, and death. I was silent, then I turned to look at Sandy, the teacher, and said, "Sandy, you don't need a professor of theology to talk to this class."

I have referred to this story many, many times in my teaching, but here, at the close of this chapter on suffering, it occurred to me that what this young girl was discussing was not simply her image of God and her feelings about God but also all the impediments to coming close to and having an experience of God's presence. Her impediments were very much like our own: disease, poverty, death, earthquakes, hurricanes, random shootings, and the rest. In retrospect today, it occurs to me that had I been as good a teacher as I should have been, I would have said to her, "So how do you get around the rocks? How do you deal with all of the obstacles to your coming to God?" From where I sit today, it would have been good to hear this wise second-grader explain how human beings cope with suffering.

What might she have said? She might have said, "Sometimes I just give up because I'm tired or because today the rocks seem too difficult to overcome." Then I might have said, "Forget about the waterfall for today at least." Or she might have said, "I could always ask my mother and father or my sisters to help me around the rocks so that it would be easier for me if we did it together." Or she might have said, "You know, I should ask my Daddy if we could just get rid of the rocks or make a path that we can get through in order to get to the waterfall much more easily."

These ways of overcoming the rocks are also ways to deal with suffering. We can simply give up, forget about the waterfall, forget about a relationship with God, and go on with our lives. Or we can work with a community to support us and help us through the difficult times. We can also work desperately hard to get rid of the obstacles—to abolish poverty, disease, and warfare—and to clear the way for our ability to experience God nearby.

I do not believe that there is an adequate theological answer to suffering. All the answers that are basically rooted in theology have not worked. The alternative is to take the whole area of suffering outside the realm of God's power. Rubenstein did this by suggesting that God had died. Kushner did this by suggesting that God just does not have the power. But then we have to deal with either an absent God or an impotent God—acknowledging all the while, of course, that all statements about God are really disguised human statements, images cast by human beings. But then we have to include our suffering in all our other relationships with God: with prayer, with the good things that happen, with the genius

of God's creation, with
the beauty of nature, and
with the immense good
that human beings can
provide.

I have long given up
on the expectation that I
can deal with the issue of
suffering on theological
grounds alone. At those
moments I feel wonder-
ful that religion is much
more than theology. At
such moments, theologi-
cal inquiry seems to hurl
me against a brick wall,

> *I do not believe that
> there is an adequate
> theological answer
> to suffering. All the
> answers that are
> basically rooted in
> theology have not
> worked.*

and if I'm going to deal with the issue of suffering
at all, I have to deal with it elsewhere. Fortunately,
the "elsewhere" in the case of Judaism includes two
extraordinarily powerful resources: community and
the liturgy and rituals for death and the suffering
that it entails.

A recent editorial comment on the shootings in
Newtown, Connecticut, during which twenty children and seven adults were killed, echoed the notion
that for many people, the most authentic response
to the tragedy was the experience of a community
of mourners. "What religion has to offer to people
at moments like this—more than theology, more
than divine presence—is community."[8] It was not

> *Even for me there are issues and experiences in life when I find my theology inadequate. Then I turn to the fact that I am a member of a community and that I have inherited a body of liturgical and ritual performances that can enrich my life in many different ways.*

God, it was certainly not theology, and it was not religious dogma that could provide a measure of relief to the mourners. Rather, they found it in the broader community of fellow mourners, friends, and family.

Community is everywhere when Jews confront suffering. The best examples are the rituals surrounding burial, shivah, mourning, *yartzheit*, and Kaddish; at the moment we confront chaos, Jewish tradition says we are never alone. The body is prepared by members of our congregation who perform the washing ritual of *taharah*. We need a minyan to say Kaddish, the prayer for the dead. During the seven days of shivah the community comes to our house. We don't go out. We are not left alone. We never mourn alone. And this is a good example of what my young student might have said about the rocks. She could have had a friend, her sister, or her parents help her negotiate the perilous journey up to the waterfall.

Jewish liturgy and ritual are also replete with ways of coping with death and the suffering that it entails. We tear our garments. We work very specifically to prepare the body for burial. We have complex rituals surrounding the mourning period. Rituals generally are ways of coping with chaos. Rituals are ordering devices; what they accomplish is to provide specific moments, specific performances, and specific spaces for us to deal with the incipient anarchy that assails us at critical moments in our life experience. We say specific words, we enter specific spaces, we observe specific moments, and we perform specific activities—many of them very different from the ones we would normally be performing in our everyday lives. The ultimate effect of all these predictabilities is on our inner lives. That is where the coping mechanism begins.

At this moment, then, I realize that as indispensable as theology is to me, it is hardly indispensable for most of the Jewish community, and even for me there are issues and experiences in life when I find my theology inadequate. Then I turn to the fact that I am a member of a community and that I have inherited a body of liturgical and ritual performances that can enrich my life in many different ways.

Ultimately, of Geertz's three challenges that the outburst of chaos poses to our attempt to order our life experiences, only the second challenge, the emotional, can be successfully accomplished in our day. The intellectual challenge is now almost exclusively in the hands of science, engineering, and technology. If and when we ultimately understand why there are earthquakes, tsunamis, airplane crashes, and even deranged murderers, then it will be because science helped us account for how these things occur, and it will also possibly help us eliminate them. As for the moral challenge, in spite of the entire history of philosophical and moral speculation, it is my conviction that we remain perplexed.

What religion can provide, however, is the resources to help us cope with the tragedies we encounter and even possibly emerge somewhat wiser.

CHAPTER 4

Death

Part of my daily morning routine is to pick up
my copy of the *New York Times*, glance at the
headlines, prepare a cup of coffee, and open the
paper to the obituary page. I do not recall when
I began my day looking at the obituary page even
before the sports section, but it has now become
routine for me. As I read the details of who died
over the past few days, the following questions
always occur to me: Why death? Why did this
person die? Why did this person die now? The
obituary frequently informs me of the specific illness that brought death, but that simply leads to
another question: Why did this person contract
this deadly illness?

89

At this point in my life, my current naturalist tendencies are overcome by my existentialist roots. (My earliest training in philosophy, as an undergraduate at McGill University, exposed me to classical existentialist literature, which had a decisive influence on my return to Judaism.) To frame the issue in existentialist terms: I know that I will die, but I need to understand why my death is built in as a part of my total life experience.

When I become even more acutely theological, I ask, Why did God create me to die? This God, who asks me every High Holy Day to pray that "God remember me for life," because this is a God who loves life and should therefore inscribe me in the Book of Life, may still determine that this will be the last High Holy Day in which I say these words. It is therefore a prayer over whose outcome I have no control.

The first mention of death in all of our classical texts occurs in chapter 2 of the book of Genesis. There, death is presented as a threat. But in chapter 3, where, after having eaten the forbidden fruit, Adam and Eve are informed that they will suffer certain punishments. Adam's will endure until he "returns to the ground"—*ad shuvcha el ha-adamah*—because, as God reminds him, "For dust you are, and to dust you shall return" (Genesis 3:19). Apparently, then, the presence of death in our world is a punishment for the sins of our ancestors.

This is the conventional interpretation of that passage in Genesis 3—certainly the canonical Christian

interpretation, which has won widespread acceptance. Other scholarly and recent interpretations
differ, suggesting that there is no mention of punishment in this text; the narrative, rather, is an attempt
to account for humanity's growing awareness of the
choices involved in adulthood and the consequences
of these choices. The reality remains that of all the
other deaths recorded in the book of Genesis—
namely those of Noah, Sarah, Abel, Abraham, Isaac,
Rebecca, Jacob, Rachel, and Joseph—none of these
deaths are punishment deaths. These personalities
are described as having died in the natural course of
events—in old age for most, in childbirth for Rachel.
There was no reason to punish any of them. The
community mourned, and continued on its communal historical journey.

In fact, throughout most of the Hebrew scriptures, death is final, with the exception of two characters: Enoch in Genesis 5:24, and Elijah in 2 Kings.
There is no mention of Elijah's death. Rather, he goes
up to heaven in a fiery chariot.

> As they were crossing, Elijah said to
> Elisha, "Tell me, what can I do for you
> before I am taken from you?" Elisha
> answered, "Let a double portion of your
> spirit pass on to me." "You have asked a
> difficult thing," he said. "If you see me
> as I am being taken from you, this will
> be granted to you; if not, it will not."

> As they kept on walking and talking, a
> fiery chariot with fiery horses suddenly
> appeared and separated one from the
> other; and Elijah went up to heaven in
> a whirlwind. Elisha saw it and he cried
> out, "Oh father, father! Israel's chariots
> and horsemen!" When he could no lon-
> ger see him, he grasped his garments and
> tore them in two.
>
> (2 KINGS 2:9–12)

Later Jewish tradition has Elijah present in the
daily liturgy, returning at every Havdalah ritual,
and joining us at every circumcision and every
Passover seder. As for Enoch, he is one of the ten
generations between Adam and Noah. All of them
lived a certain number of years, the text tells us,
and then they died. Enoch, however, lived a certain number of years and then "*v'einenu*": he was
no more.

> When Enoch had lived for sixty-five
> years, he begot Methuselah. After the
> birth of Methuselah, Enoch walked with
> God for three hundred years; and he
> begot sons and daughters. All the days of
> Enoch came to three hundred and sixty-
> five years. Enoch walked with God; then
> he was no more, for God took him.
>
> (GENESIS 5:21–24)

Yet apart from Enoch and Elijah, every person throughout Hebrew scripture dies, and the death is final.

THE AFTERLIFE IN JEWISH THOUGHT

There is only one explicit verse in Hebrew scripture that suggests that dead people can live again: Daniel 12:2.

> Many of those that sleep in the dust of the earth will awake, some to eternal life, others to reproaches, to everlasting abhorrence. And the knowledgeable will be like the bright expanse of the sky, and those who lead many to righteousness will be like the stars forever and ever.
>
> (DANIEL 12:2–3)

Chapters 10, 11, and 12 of Daniel have been widely interpreted, because they probably represent the latest stratum of Israelite literature to be accepted into the canon. Daniel 10–12 represents a coherent narrative, the centerpiece of which is his prophecy of a major war that will take place between Israel and its Syrian Greek oppressors. We now know that this war was the Maccabean war. Chapter 12 records the aftermath of the Syrian Greek oppression, when "many of those who lie in the dust of the earth will awaken" (Daniel 12:2). The reference to those who lie in the dust of the earth clearly refers back to Adam's fate in Genesis 3 and therefore to the dead. This is the first explicit reference to an afterlife in Jewish thinking, and, specifically in this context, to bodily resurrection.

A century and a half later, a second and very different notion of the afterlife appears in Jewish texts: that human beings are composed of a material body and a spiritual soul; that at death, body and soul separate; and that the body returns to the earth while the soul goes off to be with God. Because the soul is an immaterial substance, it cannot die. This dualistic view of the human being—body and soul—originated in early Greek philosophy and entered Jewish thought through the Hellenistic influences on the Jews in Alexandria. There is no reference to the eternity of the soul in scripture. In fact, there is no hint of a body-soul dualism in scripture! The Hebrew terms *nefesh* and *neshamah* do not refer to spiritual entities, but rather to the life force and the breath

> *There is only one explicit verse in Hebrew scripture that suggests that dead people can live again: Daniel 12:2.*

that vivify the material body and whose extinction means death.

As the rabbinic consensus on the afterlife emerged, these two theories—the resurrection of the body and the eternity of the soul—though apparently quite contradictory, merge. The cumulative effect, which becomes canonical in almost all of Jewish history for centuries thereafter, is that death is the separation of the body and the soul, the bodies are buried and the souls go off to God, and eventually (after the time of the coming of the Messiah) God unites each body and soul again. Then, in the original sense of identity that we possessed during our lives on Earth, we come before God in judgment.

Until Daniel 12—a very late contribution to Hebrew scripture, conventionally dated around the year 165 BCE—everybody died a terminal death. This suggests that it took the introduction of an outside notion of the afterlife to teach us something different about the inevitability of death for human beings. The fact that everybody in the Bible died, and that nobody ever suggested that any of them would live again, confirms the notion that death was just accepted as a part of the human experience.

Why did it take so long for notions of the after-life to enter Jewish experience? Perhaps our ancestors wanted to make sure that there was a major distinction between being God and being human. God lives forever; human beings die. That is why the metaphor that God died cannot be interpreted as actually referring to God; rather, it refers to our images and metaphors of God. This makes the doctrine of Richard Rubenstein far less graphic than if it actually referred to God.

For the Christian God to have died, early Christianity had to affirm that the one who died was the God who became flesh. This is also a metaphorical portrait of God—a human form of God who was crucified. God the father—the ultimate God, the God who lies beyond history and beyond all metaphors—certainly does not die. Only when God becomes human can God share the fate of all human beings to die.

It is perhaps stunning that the Christian belief in Jesus's death and resurrection has not in the least affected the evolution of Jewish thinking on bodily resurrection as a dimension of the afterlife. That notion remained canonical until the nineteenth century. This may be understood as a testimony to the profound human need to overcome the sense of the finality of death.

THE MEANING
OF DEATH

Why speculate about the meaning of death? Death is part of life. A student once said to me that the origin of death is simply birth. Because we are born, we will die. If we want to deal with the meaning of human life, we must include in our exploration the fact that all human beings eventually die. This is simply part of living. There is no mitzvah to speculate about the meaning of life, and many refuse to do it. But if we do think about the

> *We cannot read the mind of God.*

meaning of our lives, we have to take into consideration the inevitability of death. Further, if in our speculations about the meaning of human life we include God in the picture and our speculations become theological in nature, then we must also include God in the picture when we contemplate death. At this point then, we must deal with the theological issues surrounding death. And, if even righteous people die, we must conclude that the death of most of us has nothing to do with punishment. Everybody dies, regardless of the kind of life that he or she lived.

We cannot read the mind of God. Even rejecting the notion that death is punishment for sin, it remains possible to attribute various motivations to God for including death in our view of God's creation. There are two such views that people have espoused. The first is that death is a blessing—not only an "easy" death, but every death; the very *fact* of death is a blessing. Everything dies: grass and flowers, cats and dogs, leaves and trees. Death is the way nature renews and refreshes itself. Therefore, death is the universal phase in the restoration of nature so that nature can become blessed again as its cycles continue.

The second view is the opposite of death as a blessing. Death represents chaos—it is a remnant of the chaotic element of creation that God was not able to conquer at the moment of creation. That is why death is to be feared, fought, opposed, and mourned. In this view, death is a statement about the limitations of God's power.

> *Theologies of the afterlife represent our attempt to reinstitute God's power over human life.*

Theologies of the afterlife represent our attempt to reinstitute God's power over human life. We affirm that death is not terminal but merely an interim stage in God's ultimate plan for creation. We insist that everything that dies will live again. The English poet John Donne refers to this as the death of death. It is part of the Jewish eschatological dream, the culmination of history in which, among other things, all of humanity will worship the God of Israel, Israel's exile will end, peace will reign, warfare will be abolished, and death shall be no more. As Donne says:

*Death be not proud, though some
  have called thee
Mighty and dreadfull, for, thou art
  not soe,
For, those, whom thou think'st, thou
  dost overthrow,
Die not, poore death, nor yet canst
  thou kill mee.
From rest and sleepe, which but thy
  pictures bee,
Much pleasure, then from thee,
  much more must flow,
And soonest our best men with thee
  doe goe,
Rest of their bones, and soules
  deliverie.
Thou art slave to Fate, chance,
  kings, and desperate men,
And dost with poyson, warre, and
  sicknesse dwell,
And poppie, or charmes can make us
  sleepe as well,
And better then thy stroake; why
  swell'st thou then?
One short sleepe past, wee wake
  eternally,
And death shall be no more; death,
  thou shalt die.*[9]

The twentieth-century poet Dylan Thomas wrote, in "And Death Shall Have No Dominion":

> *And death shall have no dominion.*
> *Dead man naked they shall be one*
> *With the man in the wind and the*
>   *west moon;*
> *When their bones are picked clean*
>   *and the clean bones gone,*
> *They shall have stars at elbow and*
>   *foot;*
> *Though they go mad they shall be*
>   *sane,*
> *Though they sink through the sea*
>   *they shall rise again;*
> *Though lovers be lost love shall not;*
> *And death shall have no dominion.*
>
> *And death shall have no dominion.*
> *Under the windings of the sea*
> *They lying long shall not die*
>   *windily;*
> *Twisting on racks when sinews give*
>   *way,*
> *Strapped to a wheel, yet they shall*
>   *not break;*
> *Faith in their hands shall snap in*
>   *two,*

And the unicorn evils run them
  through;
Split all ends up they shan't crack;
And death shall have no dominion.

And death shall have no dominion.
No more may gulls cry at their ears
Or waves break loud on the
  seashores;
Where blew a flower may a flower
  no more
Lift its head to the blows of the rain;
Though they be mad and dead as
  nails,
Heads of the characters hammer
  through daisies;
Break in the sun till the sun breaks
  down,
And death shall have no dominion.[10]

DEATH AS CHAOS AND THE RESPONSE OF ESCHATOLOGY

I view death as one more expression of the chaotic element, what the late Milton Steinberg referred to as "the leftover scaffolding of the order of creation." There is so much in this created world that God left undone. There are hurricanes, tornadoes, and earthquakes; there is cancer and other diseases; and there are sudden accidental deaths of children of all ages. Death is one more expression of the inherent absurdity that is left over from the creation of God's world.

Remember that we are dealing with our images of God. There is a way of viewing God as ultimately benevolent, and there is a way of viewing God as ultimately malevolent or perhaps impotent. In *When Bad Things Happen to Good People*, Harold Kushner suggests that the world as a whole is trending ultimately toward the chaotic end of things and that death may simply be part of that broader picture.

> *This attempt to conquer the chaotic element in creation is the impulse that leads to eschatology.*

If this is the case, then our only legitimate human response is to fight the chaos— to fight disease, to fight the earthquake and the hurricane, to fight all the forces in the world that are part of what makes life so difficult and painful and that ultimately account for death. It is striking to me that Judaism incorporated the notion of the afterlife, that the ultimate view of death is that it too will die, and that God's power will assert itself and we will no longer speak of God as vulnerable.

This attempt to conquer the chaotic element in creation is the impulse that leads to eschatology. The term *eschatology* refers to study of the last days, the end times. The ultimate purpose of any eschatology is to try to deal with all the anomalies and absurdities that exist in historical time. Eschatology deals with how things will be when historical time has come to an end.

Jewish eschatology happens to be extraordinarily rich. It is as old as scripture and has evolved along with both the history of the Jewish people and the internal evolution of Jewish thinking about the here and now. It deals with three broad topics: what the end of time will be like for the world as a whole, what it will be like for the Jewish people, and what it will be like for the individual human being.

For the world as a whole, Jewish eschatology envisions an age of peace, the end of warfare, and the universal recognition of the Jewish people as teaching the Torah to all of humanity. For the Jewish people, it envisions the ingathering of the exiles, the return to Zion, and the rebuilding of the Temple in Jerusalem. For the individual, it envisions the death of death, the end of disease, and the end of everything that stands in the way of human fulfillment.

These are the "rocks," as my second-grade student described it, that have to be overcome if we are ultimately to stand in the aura cast by the "waterfall." Death is one of those rocks, and the various causes of death are obstacles to the age to come, when the life and fate of the Jewish people and the world as a whole will reach its ideal state. For this eschatological dream to be in place, death in the here and now cannot be a blessing. It must be one of the obstacles we have to overcome. Judaism has never glorified death. Judaism has always viewed death as a tragedy to be battled in whatever way possible. It will eventually win out in historical time, but ultimately we can dream with John Donne that death too will die.

It should be clear that the realm of eschatology is quite properly a matter of myth, in the classic academic sense of the term that I outlined earlier. It is not intended to be a factual anticipation of events that will happen in the extended future, but rather an imaginative, subjective construction of an ideal state of affairs that exists properly in the imaginations of the people who conceptualized it. It is classical wishful thinking, designed to give meaning to the course of Israelite history. It is the culminating scenario for the creation story. Creation set the world into motion; eschatology will bring it to an end. It completes the circle.

Eschatology is part of the broad frame in which cosmic history is the portrait. Portraits need a frame. What the frame does is encase the entire scope of the narrative and give it a beginning and an end. If there is no beginning and no end, then there is no middle. If there is no middle, then there is no point of focus, and the picture as a whole loses its intended meaning.

Myths effectively frame our experience. The creation myth at the beginning and the eschatological myth at the end frame the experience of history so that the entire arc of Jewish history now has a focus, an end, and a purpose. Eschatological myths are just as indispensable as creation myths are. Neither is a literal historical event. Both are imaginative constructs designed to provide meaning to the human experience as a whole.

KADDISH
D'ITCHADETA

The place to look for a statement expressing a classical theological rabbinic view on any significant issue is the liturgy. The Bible is not always trustworthy because many views are represented. The same holds for the Aggadah. But the liturgy is the work of the community as a whole. There's a collaborative, communal quality there. It reflects not an individual point of view at any given time but what the community came to believe, which in turn shapes the thinking of the worshipping community.

In Jewish liturgy there is a classic passage that recapitulates the central themes of Jewish eschatology: the *Kaddish d'Itchadeta*, the Kaddish of Renewal. Its framework is the familiar Kaddish that appears in many different places in the liturgy, but this particular Kaddish is supplemented by a paragraph that expresses everything that Jews came to believe about what would happen at the end of days, when the great renewal, the *itchadeta* (an Aramaic word from the Hebrew *chadash*) will take place. The *Kaddish d'Itchadeta* is recited, significantly, at graveside. It begins with the words of the familiar Kaddish, but continues by characterizing the Jewish view of the end of days briefly, concisely, and powerfully.

With some modifications, the *Kaddish d'Itchadeta* is also recited when we finish studying a tractate of the Talmud, as part of the *siyyum*, or closing feast that is the liturgical conclusion of a study of rabbinic text. I suspect that its inclusion at this moment reflects the rabbinic conviction that it is through the study of Torah that one achieves eternal life. Hence it belongs here, as it belongs at graveside. Here is the first part of the *Kaddish d'Itchadeta*:

> *Magnified and sanctified may His*
> *   great Name be,*
> *In the world that will in future be*
> *   renewed,*
> *Reviving the dead and raising them*
> *   up to eternal life.*
> *He will rebuild the city of Jerusalem,*
> *And in it reestablish His Temple.*
> *He will remove alien worship from*
> *   the earth*
> *And restore to its place the worship*
> *   of Heaven.*

Then the Holy One, blessed be He,
Will reign in His sovereignty and
  splendor.
May it be in your lifetime and in
  your days,
And in the lifetime of the entire
  House of Israel,
Swiftly and soon—and say: Amen.
[Congregation: May His great Name
  be blessed forever and all time.][11]

Death remains the ultimate enigma. That is precisely why we need to invoke eschatological myths to deal with it. I can, as you may have noted, engage with the issue of the existence and nature of God in a more or less coherent way. I can also discuss the theological implications of the revelation of Torah. I can also provide possibly not theological, but at least religious resources for dealing with suffering. Ultimately, however, when I deal with death, I must resort to an eschatological myth. That is probably why it took our ancestors about two thousand years to fashion the eschatological myths that inform our conversation. That is why the conclusion of this chapter leaves me with a sense of theological incompleteness. It is appropriately humbling. It provides a gentle reminder that all of theological speculation is ultimately tension filled. That is probably its greatest contribution.

Notes

1. Moses Maimonides, *Mishneh Torah*, in *A Maimonides Reader*, Isadore Twersky, ed., (Springfield, NJ: Behrman House, 1972), 45.

2. "Mind is a series of functions carried out by the brain." Interview with Charlie Rose, 2009. www.youtube.com/watch?v=rhDvWL1V_1w (accessed March 6, 2013).

3. Paul Tillich, *Dynamics of Faith* (San Francisco: HarperOne, 2001), 50.

4. Neil Gillman, *Sacred Fragments: Recovering Theology for the Modern Jew* (Philadelphia: Jewish Publication Society, 1990), 25.

5. Ibid., 32.

6. See Benjamin Sommer, "Revelation at Sinai in the Hebrew Bible and in Jewish Theology," *Journal of Religion* 79, 3 (1999): 422–451.

7. Gillman, 197.

8. Greg M. Epstein, cited in Samuel G. Freedman, "In a Crisis, Humanists Seem Absent," *New York Times*, December 29, 2012, A20.

9. John Donne, "Death Be Not Proud," www.poetryfoundation.org/poem/173363 (accessed March 10, 2013).

10. Dylan Thomas, "And Death Shall Have No Dominion," from *The Poems of Dylan Thomas* (New York: New Directions, 1943).

11. Jonathan Sacks, trans., *The Koren Siddur* (Jerusalem: Koren Publishers, 2009), 1056.

Suggestions for Further Reading

The following works have served me throughout my career in teaching, writing, and thinking about the issues covered in this book. All of them are referred to in the above pages, and readers of my other books should find them all familiar.

Fowler, James. *Stages of Faith: The Psychology of Human Development and the Quest for Meaning.* San Francisco: HarperOne, 1995.

Geertz, Clifford. *The Interpretation of Cultures.* New York: Basic Books, 1973.

Gillman, Neil. *The Death of Death: Resurrection and Immortality in Jewish Thought.* Woodstock, VT: Jewish Lights, 2000.

————. *Doing Jewish Theology: God, Torah and Israel in Modern Judaism.* Woodstock, VT: Jewish Lights, 2004.

————. *Sacred Fragments: Recovering Theology for the Modern Jew.* Philadelphia: Jewish Publication Society, 1990.

————. *Traces of God: Seeing God in Torah, History and Everyday Life*. Woodstock, VT: Jewish Lights, 2006.

————. *The Way Into Encountering God in Judaism*. Woodstock, VT: Jewish Lights, 2004.

Glatzer, Nahum. *The Dimensions of Job*. New York: Schocken Books, 1969.

Green, Arthur. *Radical Judaism: Rethinking God and Tradition*. New Haven, CT: Yale University Press, 2010.

Greenberg, Irving. "Cloud of Smoke, Pillar of Fire: Judaism, Christianity, Modernity after the Holocaust," in *Auschwitz: Beginning of a New Era? Reflections on the Holocaust. Papers Given at the International Symposium on the Holocaust, Held at the Cathedral of Saint John the Divine,* ed. Eva Fleischner, New York: Ktav Publishers, 1977.

————."Theology after the Shoah: The Transformation of the Core Paradigm." *Modern Judaism* 26, 3 (2006): 213–239.

Herberg, Will. *Judaism and Modern Man*. New York: Antheneum, 1970.

Heschel, Abraham Joshua. *God in Search of Man: A Philosophy of Judaism*. New York: Farrar, Straus and Giroux, 1976.

————. *The Prophets*. New York: Harper Perennial, 2001.

Kaplan, Mordecai. *Questions Jews Ask: Reconstructionist Answers*. Jenkintown, PA: Reconstructionist Press, 1966.

Kushner, Harold. *When Bad Things Happen to Good People*. New York: Anchor, 2004.

Plaskow, Judith. *Standing Again at Sinai: Judaism from a Feminist Perspective*. New York: Harper Collins, 1991.

Rosenzweig, Franz. *On Jewish Learning*. Madison, WI: University of Wisconsin Press, 2002.

Sommer, Benjamin. *The Bodies of God and the World of Ancient Israel*. Boston: Cambridge University Press, 2011.

———. "Revelation at Sinai in the Hebrew Bible and in Jewish Theology." *Journal of Religion* 79, 3 (1999): 422–451.

Tillich, Paul. *Dynamics of Faith*. San Francisco: HarperOne, 2001.

Wiman, Christopher. *My Bright Abyss: Meditation of a Modern Believer*. New York: Farrar, Straus and Giroux, 2013.

Bible Study / Midrash

Passing Life's Tests: Spiritual Reflections on the Trial of Abraham, the Binding of Isaac   *By Rabbi Bradley Shavit Artson, DHL*
Invites us to use this powerful tale as a tool for our own soul wrestling, to confront our existential sacrifices and enable us to face—and surmount—life's tests.
6 x 9, 176 pp, Quality PB, 978-1-58023-631-7   **$18.99**

The Messiah and the Jews: Three Thousand Years of Tradition, Belief and Hope   *By Rabbi Elaine Rose Glickman; Foreword by Rabbi Neil Gillman, PhD; Preface by Rabbi Judith Z. Abrams, PhD*
Explores and explains an astonishing range of primary and secondary sources, infusing them with new meaning for the modern reader.
6 x 9, 192 pp, Quality PB, 978-1-58023-690-4   **$16.99**

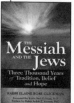

Speaking Torah: Spiritual Teachings from around the Maggid's Table—in Two Volumes   *By Arthur Green, with Ebn Leader, Ariel Evan Mayse and Or N. Rose*
The most powerful Hasidic teachings made accessible—from some of the world's preeminent authorities on Jewish thought and spirituality.
Volume 1—6 x 9, 512 pp, Hardcover, 978-1-58023-668-3   **$34.99**
Volume 2—6 x 9, 448 pp, Hardcover, 978-1-58023-694-2   **$34.99**

Masking and Unmasking Ourselves: Interpreting Biblical Texts on Clothing & Identity   *By Dr. Norman J. Cohen*
Presents ten Bible stories that involve clothing in an essential way, as a means of learning about the text, its characters and their interactions.
6 x 9, 240 pp, HC, 978-1-58023-461-0   **$24.99**

The Genesis of Leadership: What the Bible Teaches Us about Vision, Values and Leading Change   *By Rabbi Nathan Laufer; Foreword by Senator Joseph I. Lieberman*
6 x 9, 288 pp, Quality PB, 978-1-58023-352-1   **$18.99**

Hineini in Our Lives: Learning How to Respond to Others through 14 Biblical Texts and Personal Stories   *By Rabbi Norman J. Cohen, PhD*   6 x 9, 240 pp, Quality PB, 978-1-58023-274-6   **$16.99**

The Modern Men's Torah Commentary: New Insights from Jewish Men on the 54 Weekly Torah Portions   *Edited by Rabbi Jeffrey K. Salkin*
6 x 9, 368 pp, HC, 978-1-58023-395-8   **$24.99**

Moses and the Journey to Leadership: Timeless Lessons of Effective Management from the Bible and Today's Leaders   *By Rabbi Norman J. Cohen, PhD*
6 x 9, 240 pp, Quality PB, 978-1-58023-351-4   **$18.99**; HC, 978-1-58023-227-2   **$21.99**

The Other Talmud—*The Yerushalmi*: Unlocking the Secrets of The Talmud of Israel for Judaism Today   *By Rabbi Judith Z. Abrams, PhD*
6 x 9, 256 pp, HC, 978-1-58023-463-4   **$24.99**

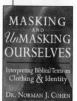

Sage Tales: Wisdom and Wonder from the Rabbis of the Talmud
By Rabbi Burton L. Visotzky   6 x 9, 256 pp, HC, 978-1-58023-456-6   **$24.99**

The Torah Revolution: Fourteen Truths That Changed the World
By Rabbi Reuven Hammer, PhD   6 x 9, 240 pp, HC, 978-1-58023-457-3   **$24.99**

The Wisdom of Judaism: An Introduction to the Values of the Talmud
By Rabbi Dov Peretz Elkins   6 x 9, 192 pp, Quality PB, 978-1-58023-327-9   **$16.99**

Bar / Bat Mitzvah

The Mitzvah Project Book
Making Mitzvah Part of Your Bar/Bat Mitzvah ... and Your Life
By Liz Suneby and Diane Heiman; Foreword by Rabbi Jeffrey K. Salkin; Preface by Rabbi Sharon Brous
The go-to source for Jewish young adults and their families looking to make the
world a better place through good deeds—big or small.
6 x 9, 224 pp, Quality PB Original, 978-1-58023-458-0 **$16.99** *For ages 11–13*

The Bar/Bat Mitzvah Memory Book, 2nd Edition: An Album for Treasuring
the Spiritual Celebration
By Rabbi Jeffrey K. Salkin and Nina Salkin
8 x 10, 48 pp, 2-color text, Deluxe HC, ribbon marker, 978-1-58023-263-0 **$19.99**

For Kids—Putting God on Your Guest List, 2nd Edition: How to Claim the
Spiritual Meaning of Your Bar or Bat Mitzvah *By Rabbi Jeffrey K. Salkin*
6 x 9, 144 pp, Quality PB, 978-1-58023-308-8 **$15.99** *For ages 11–13*

The Jewish Prophet: Visionary Words from Moses and Miriam to Henrietta Szold
and A. J. Heschel *By Rabbi Dr. Michael J. Shire*
6½ x 8½, 128 pp, 123 full-color illus., HC, 978-1-58023-168-8 **$14.95**

Putting God on the Guest List, 3rd Edition: How to Reclaim the Spiritual
Meaning of Your Child's Bar or Bat Mitzvah *By Rabbi Jeffrey K. Salkin*
6 x 9, 224 pp, Quality PB, 978-1-58023-222-7 **$16.99**

Putting God on the Guest List Teacher's Guide
8½ x 11, 48 pp, PB, 978-1-58023-226-5 **$8.99**

Teens / Young Adults

Text Messages: A Torah Commentary for Teens
Edited by Rabbi Jeffrey K. Salkin
Shows today's teens how each Torah portion contains worlds of meaning for
them, for what they are going through in their lives, and how they can shape their
Jewish identity as they enter adulthood.
6 x 9, 304 pp (est), HC, 978-1-58023-507-5 **$24.99**

Hannah Senesh: Her Life and Diary, the First Complete Edition
By Hannah Senesh; Foreword by Marge Piercy; Preface by Eitan Senesh; Afterword by Roberta Grossman
6 x 9, 368 pp, b/w photos, Quality PB, 978-1-58023-342-2 **$19.99**

I Am Jewish: Personal Reflections Inspired by the Last Words of Daniel Pearl
Edited by Judea and Ruth Pearl 6 x 9, 304 pp, Deluxe PB w/ flaps, 978-1-58023-259-3 **$19.99**
Download a free copy of the *I Am Jewish Teacher's Guide* at www.jewishlights.com.

The JGirl's Guide: The Young Jewish Woman's Handbook for Coming of Age
By Penina Adelman, Ali Feldman and Shulamit Reinharz
6 x 9, 240 pp, Quality PB, 978-1-58023-215-9 **$14.99** *For ages 11 & up*

The JGirl's Teacher's and Parent's Guide
8½ x 11, 56 pp, PB, 978-1-58023-225-8 **$8.99**

Tough Questions Jews Ask, 2nd Edition: A Young Adult's Guide to Building a
Jewish Life *By Rabbi Edward Feinstein*
6 x 9, 160 pp, Quality PB, 978-1-58023-454-2 **$16.99** *For ages 11 & up*

Tough Questions Jews Ask Teacher's Guide
8½ x 11, 72 pp, PB, 978-1-58023-187-9 **$8.95**

Pre-Teens

Be Like God: God's To-Do List for Kids
By Dr. Ron Wolfson
Encourages kids ages eight through twelve to use their God-given superpowers
to find the many ways they can make a difference in the lives of others and find
meaning and purpose for their own.
7 x 9, 144 pp, Quality PB, 978-1-58023-510-5 **$15.99** *For ages 8–12*

The Book of Miracles: A Young Person's Guide to Jewish Spiritual Awareness
By Lawrence Kushner, with all-new illustrations by the author.
6 x 9, 96 pp, 2-color illus., HC, 978-1-879045-78-1 **$16.95** *For ages 9–13*

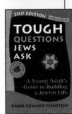

Congregation Resources

Jewish Megatrends: Charting the Course of the American Jewish Future
By Rabbi Sidney Schwarz; Foreword by Ambassador Stuart E. Eizenstat
Visionary solutions for a community ripe for transformational change—from fourteen leading innovators of Jewish life.
6 x 9, 288 pp, HC, 978-1-58023-667-6 **$24.99**

Relational Judaism: Using the Power of Relationships to Transform the Jewish Community *By Dr. Ron Wolfson*
How to transform the model of twentieth-century Jewish institutions into twenty-first-century relational communities offering meaning and purpose, belonging and blessing.
6 x 9, 288 pp, HC, 978-1-58023-666-9 **$24.99**

Revolution of Jewish Spirit: How to Revive *Ruakh* in Your Spiritual Life, Transform Your Synagogue & Inspire Your Jewish Community
By Rabbi Baruch HaLevi, DMin, and Ellen Frankel, LCSW; Foreword by Dr. Ron Wolfson
A practical and engaging guide to reinvigorating Jewish life. Offers strategies for sustaining and expanding transformation, impassioned leadership, inspired programming and inviting sacred spaces.
6 x 9, 224 pp, Quality PB Original, 978-1-58023-625-6 **$19.99**

Building a Successful Volunteer Culture: Finding Meaning in Service in the Jewish Community *By Rabbi Charles Simon; Foreword by Shelley Lindauer; Preface by Dr. Ron Wolfson*
6 x 9, 192 pp, Quality PB, 978-1-58023-408-5 **$16.99**

The Case for Jewish Peoplehood: Can We Be One?
By Dr. Erica Brown and Dr. Misha Galperin; Foreword by Rabbi Joseph Telushkin
6 x 9, 224 pp, HC, 978-1-58023-401-6 **$21.99**

Empowered Judaism: What Independent Minyanim Can Teach Us about Building Vibrant Jewish Communities *By Rabbi Elie Kaunfer; Foreword by Prof. Jonathan D. Sarna*
6 x 9, 224 pp, Quality PB, 978-1-58023-412-2 **$18.99**

Finding a Spiritual Home: How a New Generation of Jews Can Transform the American Synagogue *By Rabbi Sidney Schwarz*
6 x 9, 352 pp, Quality PB, 978-1-58023-185-5 **$19.95**

Inspired Jewish Leadership: Practical Approaches to Building Strong Communities
By Dr. Erica Brown 6 x 9, 256 pp, HC, 978-1-58023-361-3 **$27.99**

Jewish Pastoral Care, 2nd Edition: A Practical Handbook from Traditional & Contemporary Sources *Edited by Rabbi Dayle A. Friedman, MSW, MAJCS, BCC*
6 x 9, 528 pp, Quality PB, 978-1-58023-427-6 **$35.00**

Jewish Spiritual Direction: An Innovative Guide from Traditional and Contemporary Sources
Edited by Rabbi Howard A. Addison, PhD, and Barbara Eve Breitman, MSW
6 x 9, 368 pp, HC, 978-1-58023-230-2 **$30.00**

A Practical Guide to Rabbinic Counseling
Edited by Rabbi Yisrael N. Levitz, PhD, and Rabbi Abraham J. Twerski, MD
6 x 9, 432 pp, HC, 978-1-58023-562-4 **$40.00**

Professional Spiritual & Pastoral Care: A Practical Clergy and Chaplain's Handbook
Edited by Rabbi Stephen B. Roberts, MBA, MHL, BCJC
6 x 9, 480 pp, HC, 978-1-59473-312-3 **$50.00**

Reimagining Leadership in Jewish Organizations: Ten Practical Lessons to Help You Implement Change and Achieve Your Goals *By Dr. Misha Galperin*
6 x 9, 192 pp, Quality PB, 978-1-58023-492-4 **$16.99**

Rethinking Synagogues: A New Vocabulary for Congregational Life
By Rabbi Lawrence A. Hoffman, PhD 6 x 9, 240 pp, Quality PB, 978-1-58023-248-7 **$19.99**

Spiritual Community: The Power to Restore Hope, Commitment and Joy
By Rabbi David A. Teutsch, PhD
5½ x 8½, 144 pp, HC, 978-1-58023-270-8 **$19.99**

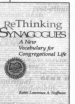

Spiritual Boredom: Rediscovering the Wonder of Judaism *By Dr. Erica Brown*
6 x 9, 208 pp, HC, 978-1-58023-405-4 **$21.99**

The Spirituality of Welcoming: How to Transform Your Congregation into a Sacred Community *By Dr. Ron Wolfson* 6 x 9, 224 pp, Quality PB, 978-1-58023-244-9 **$19.99**

Meditation

The Magic of Hebrew Chant: Healing the Spirit, Transforming the Mind, Deepening Love
By Rabbi Shefa Gold; Foreword by Sylvia Boorstein
Introduces this transformative spiritual practice as a way to unlock the power of sacred texts and make prayer and meditation the delight of your life. Includes musical notations. 6 x 9, 352 pp, Quality PB, 978-1-58023-671-3 **$24.99**

The Magic of Hebrew Chant Companion—The Big Book of Musical Notations and Incantations
8½ x 11, 154 pp, PB, 978-1-58023-722-2 **$19.99**

Jewish Meditation Practices for Everyday Life
Awakening Your Heart, Connecting with God
By Rabbi Jeff Roth
Offers a fresh take on meditation that draws on life experience and living life with greater clarity as opposed to the traditional method of rigorous study.
6 x 9, 224 pp, Quality PB, 978-1-58023-397-2 **$18.99**

Discovering Jewish Meditation, 2nd Edition
Instruction & Guidance for Learning an Ancient Spiritual Practice
By Nan Fink Gefen, PhD 6 x 9, 208 pp, Quality PB, 978-1-58023-462-7 **$16.99**

The Handbook of Jewish Meditation Practices
A Guide for Enriching the Sabbath and Other Days of Your Life
By Rabbi David A. Cooper 6 x 9, 208 pp, Quality PB, 978-1-58023-102-2 **$16.95**

Meditation from the Heart of Judaism
Today's Teachers Share Their Practices, Techniques, and Faith
Edited by Avram Davis 6 x 9, 256 pp, Quality PB, 978-1-58023-049-0 **$16.95**

Discovering
Jewish
Meditation

Instruction & Guidance
for Learning an
Ancient Spiritual Practice

NAN FINK GEFEN, PhD

Ritual / Sacred Practices

God in Your Body: Kabbalah, Mindfulness and Embodied Spiritual Practice
By Jay Michaelson
The first comprehensive treatment of the body in Jewish spiritual practice and an essential guide to the sacred. 6 x 9, 272 pp, Quality PB, 978-1-58023-304-0 **$18.99**

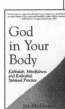

The Book of Jewish Sacred Practices: CLAL's Guide to Everyday & Holiday Rituals & Blessings *Edited by Rabbi Irwin Kula and Vanessa L. Ochs, PhD*
6 x 9, 368 pp, Quality PB, 978-1-58023-152-7 **$18.95**

The Jewish Dream Book: The Key to Opening the Inner Meaning of Your Dreams
By Vanessa L. Ochs, PhD, with Elizabeth Ochs; Illus. by Kristina Swarner
8 x 8, 128 pp, Full-color illus., Deluxe PB w/ flaps, 978-1-58023-132-9 $16.95

Jewish Ritual: A Brief Introduction for Christians
By Rabbi Kerry M. Olitzky and Rabbi Daniel Judson
5½ x 8½, 144 pp, Quality PB, 978-1-58023-210-4 **$14.99**

The Rituals & Practices of a Jewish Life: A Handbook for Personal Spiritual Renewal *Edited by Rabbi Kerry M. Olitzky and Rabbi Daniel Judson*
6 x 9, 272 pp, Illus., Quality PB, 978-1-58023-169-5 **$18.95**

The Sacred Art of Lovingkindness: Preparing to Practice
By Rabbi Rami Shapiro 5½ x 8½, 176 pp, Quality PB, 978-1-59473-151-8 **$16.99**
(A book from SkyLight Paths, Jewish Lights' sister imprint)

Mystery & Detective Fiction

Criminal Kabbalah: An Intriguing Anthology of Jewish Mystery & Detective Fiction *Edited by Lawrence W. Raphael; Foreword by Laurie R. King*
All-new stories from twelve of today's masters of mystery and detective fiction—sure to delight mystery buffs of all faith traditions.
6 x 9, 256 pp, Quality PB, 978-1-58023-109-1 **$16.95**

Mystery Midrash: An Anthology of Jewish Mystery & Detective Fiction
Edited by Lawrence W. Raphael; Preface by Joel Siegel
6 x 9, 304 pp, Quality PB, 978-1-58023-055-1 **$16.95**

Life Cycle

Marriage / Parenting / Family / Aging

The New Jewish Baby Album: Creating and Celebrating the Beginning of a Spiritual Life—A Jewish Lights Companion
By the Editors at Jewish Lights; Foreword by Anita Diamant; Preface by Rabbi Sandy Eisenberg Sasso
A spiritual keepsake that will be treasured for generations. More than just a memory book, *shows you how—and why it's important*—to create a Jewish home and a Jewish life. 8 x 10, 64 pp, Deluxe Padded HC, Full-color illus., 978-1-58023-138-1 **$19.95**

The Jewish Pregnancy Book: A Resource for the Soul, Body & Mind during Pregnancy, Birth & the First Three Months *By Sandy Falk, MD, and Rabbi Daniel Judson, with Steven A. Rapp* Medical information, prayers and rituals for each stage of pregnancy. 7 x 10, 208 pp, b/w photos, Quality PB, 978-1-58023-178-7 **$16.95**

Celebrating Your New Jewish Daughter: Creating Jewish Ways to Welcome Baby Girls into the Covenant—New and Traditional Ceremonies *By Debra Nussbaum Cohen; Foreword by Rabbi Sandy Eisenberg Sasso* 6 x 9, 272 pp, Quality PB, 978-1-58023-090-2 **$18.95**

The New Jewish Baby Book, 2nd Edition: Names, Ceremonies & Customs—A Guide for Today's Families *By Anita Diamant* 6 x 9, 320 pp, Quality PB, 978-1-58023-251-7 **$19.99**

Parenting as a Spiritual Journey: Deepening Ordinary and Extraordinary Events into Sacred Occasions *By Rabbi Nancy Fuchs-Kreimer, PhD*
6 x 9, 224 pp, Quality PB, 978-1-58023-016-2 **$17.99**

Parenting Jewish Teens: A Guide for the Perplexed
By Joanne Doades Explores the questions and issues that shape the world in which today's Jewish teenagers live and offers constructive advice to parents.
6 x 9, 176 pp, Quality PB, 978-1-58023-305-7 **$16.99**

Judaism for Two: A Spiritual Guide for Strengthening and Celebrating Your Loving Relationship *By Rabbi Nancy Fuchs-Kreimer, PhD, and Rabbi Nancy H. Wiener, DMin; Foreword by Rabbi Elliot N. Dorff, PhD*
Addresses the ways Jewish teachings can enhance and strengthen committed relationships. 6 x 9, 224 pp, Quality PB, 978-1-58023-254-8 **$16.99**

The Creative Jewish Wedding Book, 2nd Edition: A Hands-On Guide to New & Old Traditions, Ceremonies & Celebrations *By Gabrielle Kaplan-Mayer*
9 x 9, 288 pp, b/w photos, Quality PB, 978-1-58023-398-9 **$19.99**

Divorce Is a Mitzvah: A Practical Guide to Finding Wholeness and Holiness When Your Marriage Dies *By Rabbi Perry Netter; Afterword by Rabbi Laura Geller*
6 x 9, 224 pp, Quality PB, 978-1-58023-172-5 **$16.95**

Embracing the Covenant: Converts to Judaism Talk About Why & How
By Rabbi Allan Berkowitz and Patti Moskovitz 6 x 9, 192 pp, Quality PB, 978-1-879045-50-7 **$16.95**

The Guide to Jewish Interfaith Family Life: An InterfaithFamily.com Handbook
Edited by Ronnie Friedland and Edmund Case
6 x 9, 384 pp, Quality PB, 978-1-58023-153-4 **$18.95**

A Heart of Wisdom: Making the Jewish Journey from Midlife through the Elder Years
Edited by Susan Berrin; Foreword by Rabbi Harold Kushner
6 x 9, 384 pp, Quality PB, 978-1-58023-051-3 **$18.95**

Introducing My Faith and My Community: The Jewish Outreach Institute Guide for the Christian in a Jewish Interfaith Relationship
By Rabbi Kerry M. Olitzky 6 x 9, 176 pp, Quality PB, 978-1-58023-192-3 **$16.99**

Making a Successful Jewish Interfaith Marriage: The Jewish Outreach Institute Guide to Opportunities, Challenges and Resources *By Rabbi Kerry M. Olitzky with Joan Peterson Littman*
6 x 9, 176 pp, Quality PB, 978-1-58023-170-1 **$16.95**

A Man's Responsibility: A Jewish Guide to Being a Son, a Partner in Marriage, a Father and a Community Leader *By Rabbi Joseph B. Meszler*
6 x 9, 192 pp, Quality PB, 978-1-58023-435-1 **$16.99**

So That Your Values Live On: Ethical Wills and How to Prepare Them
Edited by Rabbi Jack Riemer and Rabbi Nathaniel Stampfer
6 x 9, 272 pp, Quality PB, 978-1-879045-34-7 **$18.99**

Holidays / Holy Days

Prayers of Awe Series

An exciting new series that examines the High Holy Day liturgy to enrich the praying experience of everyone—whether experienced worshipers or guests who encounter Jewish prayer for the very first time.

We Have Sinned—Sin and Confession in Judaism: *Ashamnu* and *Al Chet*
Edited by Rabbi Lawrence A. Hoffman, PhD
A varied and fascinating look at sin, confession and pardon in Judaism, as suggested by the centrality of *Ashamnu* and *Al Chet*, two prayers that people know so well, though understand so little. 6 x 9, 304 pp, HC, 978-1-58023-612-6 **$24.99**

Who by Fire, Who by Water—*Un'taneh Tokef*
Edited by Rabbi Lawrence A. Hoffman, PhD
6 x 9, 272 pp, Quality PB, 978-1-58023-672-0 **$19.99**; HC, 978-1-58023-424-5 **$24.99**

All These Vows—*Kol Nidre*
Edited by Rabbi Lawrence A. Hoffman, PhD 6 x 9, 288 pp, HC, 978-1-58023-430-6 **$24.99**

Rosh Hashanah Readings: Inspiration, Information and Contemplation
Yom Kippur Readings: Inspiration, Information and Contemplation
Edited by Rabbi Dov Peretz Elkins; Section Introductions from Arthur Green's These Are the Words
Rosh Hashanah: 6 x 9, 400 pp, Quality PB, 978-1-58023-437-5 **$19.99**
Yom Kippur: 6 x 9, 368 pp, Quality PB, 978-1-58023-438-2 **$19.99**; HC, 978-1-58023-271-5 **$24.99**

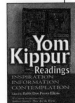

Reclaiming Judaism as a Spiritual Practice: Holy Days and Shabbat
By Rabbi Goldie Milgram 7 x 9, 272 pp, Quality PB, 978-1-58023-205-0 **$19.99**

The Sabbath Soul: Mystical Reflections on the Transformative Power of Holy Time
Selection, Translation and Commentary by Eitan Fishbane, PhD
6 x 9, 208 pp, Quality PB, 978-1-58023-459-7 **$18.99**

Shabbat, 2nd Edition: The Family Guide to Preparing for and Celebrating the Sabbath
By Dr. Ron Wolfson 7 x 9, 320 pp, Illus., Quality PB, 978-1-58023-164-0 **$19.99**

Hanukkah, 2nd Edition: The Family Guide to Spiritual Celebration
By Dr. Ron Wolfson 7 x 9, 240 pp, Illus., Quality PB, 978-1-58023-122-0 **$18.95**

Passover

My People's Passover Haggadah
Traditional Texts, Modern Commentaries
Edited by Rabbi Lawrence A. Hoffman, PhD, and David Arnow, PhD
A diverse and exciting collection of commentaries on the traditional Passover Haggadah—in two volumes!
Vol. 1: 7 x 10, 304 pp, HC, 978-1-58023-354-5 **$24.99**
Vol. 2: 7 x 10, 320 pp, HC, 978-1-58023-346-0 **$24.99**

Freedom Journeys: The Tale of Exodus and Wilderness across Millennia
By Rabbi Arthur O. Waskow and Rabbi Phyllis O. Berman
Explores how the story of Exodus echoes in our own time, calling us to relearn and rethink the Passover story through social-justice, ecological, feminist and interfaith perspectives. 6 x 9, 288 pp, HC, 978-1-58023-445-0 **$24.99**

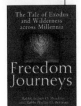

Leading the Passover Journey: The Seder's Meaning Revealed, the Haggadah's Story Retold *By Rabbi Nathan Laufer*
Uncovers the hidden meaning of the Seder's rituals and customs.
6 x 9, 224 pp, Quality PB, 978-1-58023-399-6 **$18.99**

Creating Lively Passover Seders, 2nd Edition: A Sourcebook of Engaging Tales, Texts & Activities *By David Arnow, PhD* 7 x 9, 464 pp, Quality PB, 978-1-58023-444-3 **$24.99**

Passover, 2nd Edition: The Family Guide to Spiritual Celebration
By Dr. Ron Wolfson with Joel Lurie Grishaver 7 x 9, 416 pp, Quality PB, 978-1-58023-174-9 **$19.95**

The Women's Passover Companion: Women's Reflections on the Festival of Freedom
Edited by Rabbi Sharon Cohen Anisfeld, Tara Mohr and Catherine Spector; Foreword by Paula E. Hyman
6 x 9, 352 pp, Quality PB, 978-1-58023-231-9 **$19.99**; HC, 978-1-58023-128-2 **$24.95**

The Women's Seder Sourcebook: Rituals & Readings for Use at the Passover Seder
Edited by Rabbi Sharon Cohen Anisfeld, Tara Mohr and Catherine Spector
6 x 9, 384 pp, Quality PB, 978-1-58023-232-6 **$19.99**

Social Justice

Where Justice Dwells
A Hands-On Guide to Doing Social Justice in Your Jewish Community
By Rabbi Jill Jacobs; Foreword by Rabbi David Saperstein
Provides ways to envision and act on your own ideals of social justice.
7 x 9, 288 pp, Quality PB Original, 978-1-58023-453-5 **$24.99**

There Shall Be No Needy
Pursuing Social Justice through Jewish Law and Tradition
By Rabbi Jill Jacobs; Foreword by Rabbi Elliot N. Dorff, PhD; Preface by Simon Greer
Confronts the most pressing issues of twenty-first-century America from a deeply Jewish perspective. 6 x 9, 288 pp, Quality PB, 978-1-58023-425-2 **$16.99**

There Shall Be No Needy Teacher's Guide 8½ x 11, 56 pp, PB, 978-1-58023-429-0 **$8.99**

Conscience
The Duty to Obey and the Duty to Disobey
By Rabbi Harold M. Schulweis
Examines the idea of conscience and the role conscience plays in our relationships to government, law, ethics, religion, human nature, God—and to each other.
6 x 9, 160 pp, Quality PB, 978-1-58023-419-1 **$16.99**; HC, 978-1-58023-375-0 **$19.99**

Judaism and Justice
The Jewish Passion to Repair the World
By Rabbi Sidney Schwarz; Foreword by Ruth Messinger
Explores the relationship between Judaism, social justice and the Jewish identity of American Jews. 6 x 9, 352 pp, Quality PB, 978-1-58023-353-8 **$19.99**

Spirituality / Women's Interest

New Jewish Feminism
Probing the Past, Forging the Future
Edited by Rabbi Elyse Goldstein; Foreword by Anita Diamant
Looks at the growth and accomplishments of Jewish feminism and what they mean for Jewish women today and tomorrow.
6 x 9, 480 pp, HC, 978-1-58023-359-0 **$24.99**

The Divine Feminine in Biblical Wisdom Literature
Selections Annotated & Explained
Translation & Annotation by Rabbi Rami Shapiro
5½ x 8½, 240 pp, Quality PB, 978-1-59473-109-9 **$16.99**
(A book from SkyLight Paths, Jewish Lights' sister imprint)

The Quotable Jewish Woman
Wisdom, Inspiration & Humor from the Mind & Heart
Edited by Elaine Bernstein Partnow
6 x 9, 496 pp, Quality PB, 978-1-58023-236-4 **$19.99**

The Women's Haftarah Commentary
New Insights from Women Rabbis on the 54 Weekly Haftarah Portions, the 5 Megillot & Special Shabbatot
Edited by Rabbi Elyse Goldstein
Illuminates the historical significance of female portrayals in the Haftarah and the Five Megillot. 6 x 9, 560 pp, Quality PB, 978-1-58023-371-2 **$19.99**

The Women's Torah Commentary
New Insights from Women Rabbis on the 54 Weekly Torah Portions
Edited by Rabbi Elyse Goldstein
Over fifty women rabbis offer inspiring insights on the Torah, in a week-by-week format.
6 x 9, 496 pp, Quality PB, 978-1-58023-370-5 **$19.99**; HC, 978-1-58023-076-6 **$34.95**

See Passover for *The Women's Passover Companion: Women's Reflections on the Festival of Freedom* and *The Women's Seder Sourcebook: Rituals & Readings for Use at the Passover Seder.*

Theology / Philosophy / The Way Into... Series

The Way Into... series offers an accessible and highly usable "guided tour" of the Jewish faith, people, history and beliefs—in total, an introduction to Judaism that will enable you to understand and interact with the sacred texts of the Jewish tradition. Each volume is written by a leading contemporary scholar and teacher, and explores one key aspect of Judaism. The Way Into... series enables all readers to achieve a real sense of Jewish cultural literacy through guided study.

The Way Into Encountering God in Judaism
By Rabbi Neil Gillman, PhD
For everyone who wants to understand how Jews have encountered God throughout history and today.
6 x 9, 240 pp, Quality PB, 978-1-58023-199-2 **$18.99**; HC, 978-1-58023-025-4 **$21.95**
Also Available: **The Jewish Approach to God:** A Brief Introduction for Christians
By Rabbi Neil Gillman, PhD
5½ x 8½, 192 pp, Quality PB, 978-1-58023-190-9 **$16.95**

The Way Into Jewish Mystical Tradition
By Rabbi Lawrence Kushner
Allows readers to interact directly with the sacred mystical texts of the Jewish tradition. An accessible introduction to the concepts of Jewish mysticism, their religious and spiritual significance, and how they relate to life today.
6 x 9, 224 pp, Quality PB, 978-1-58023-200-5 **$18.99**

The Way Into Jewish Prayer
By Rabbi Lawrence A. Hoffman, PhD
Opens the door to 3,000 years of Jewish prayer, making anyone feel at home in the Jewish way of communicating with God.
6 x 9, 208 pp, Quality PB, 978-1-58023-201-2 **$18.99**

The Way Into Jewish Prayer Teacher's Guide
By Rabbi Jennifer Ossakow Goldsmith
8½ x 11, 42 pp, PB, 978-1-58023-345-3 **$8.99**
Download a free copy at www.jewishlights.com.

The Way Into Judaism and the Environment
By Jeremy Benstein, PhD
Explores the ways in which Judaism contributes to contemporary social-environmental issues, the extent to which Judaism is part of the problem and how it can be part of the solution.
6 x 9, 288 pp, Quality PB, 978-1-58023-368-2 **$18.99**; HC, 978-1-58023-268-5 **$24.99**

The Way Into *Tikkun Olam* (Repairing the World)
By Rabbi Elliot N. Dorff, PhD
An accessible introduction to the Jewish concept of the individual's responsibility to care for others and repair the world.
6 x 9, 304 pp, Quality PB, 978-1-58023-328-6 **$18.99**

The Way Into Torah
By Rabbi Norman J. Cohen, PhD
Helps guide you in the exploration of the origins and development of Torah, explains why it should be studied and how to do it.
6 x 9, 176 pp, Quality PB, 978-1-58023-198-5 **$16.95**

The Way Into the Varieties of Jewishness
By Sylvia Barack Fishman, PhD
Explores the religious and historical understanding of what it has meant to be Jewish from ancient times to the present controversy over "Who is a Jew?"
6 x 9, 288 pp, Quality PB, 978-1-58023-367-5 **$18.99**; HC, 978-1-58023-030-8 **$24.99**

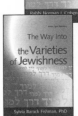

Spirituality

Amazing Chesed: Living a Grace-Filled Judaism
By Rabbi Rami Shapiro
Drawing from ancient and contemporary, traditional and non-traditional Jewish wisdom, reclaims the idea of grace in Judaism.
6 x 9, 176 pp, Quality PB, 978-1-58023-624-9 **$16.99**

Jewish with Feeling: A Guide to Meaningful Jewish Practice
By Rabbi Zalman Schachter-Shalomi with Joel Segel
Takes off from basic questions like "Why be Jewish?" and whether the word God still speaks to us today and lays out a vision for a whole-person Judaism.
5½ x 8½, 288 pp, Quality PB, 978-1-58023-691-1 **$19.99**

The Jewish Lights Spirituality Handbook: A Guide to Understanding, Exploring & Living a Spiritual Life *Edited by Stuart M. Matlins*
What exactly is "Jewish" about spirituality? How do I make it a part of my life? Fifty of today's foremost spiritual leaders share their ideas and experience with us.
6 x 9, 456 pp, Quality PB, 978-1-58023-093-3 **$19.99**

Aleph-Bet Yoga: Embodying the Hebrew Letters for Physical and Spiritual Well-Being
By Steven A. Rapp; Foreword by Tamar Frankiel, PhD, and Judy Greenfeld; Preface by Hart Lazer
7 x 10, 128 pp, b/w photos, Quality PB, Lay-flat binding, 978-1-58023-162-6 **$16.95**

A Book of Life: Embracing Judaism as a Spiritual Practice
By Rabbi Michael Strassfeld 6 x 9, 544 pp, Quality PB, 978-1-58023-247-0 **$19.99**

Bringing the Psalms to Life: How to Understand and Use the Book of Psalms
By Rabbi Daniel F. Polish, PhD 6 x 9, 208 pp, Quality PB, 978-1-58023-157-2 **$16.95**

Does the Soul Survive? A Jewish Journey to Belief in Afterlife, Past Lives & Living with Purpose *By Rabbi Elie Kaplan Spitz; Foreword by Brian L. Weiss, MD*
6 x 9, 288 pp, Quality PB, 978-1-58023-165-7 **$18.99**

Entering the Temple of Dreams: Jewish Prayers, Movements and Meditations for the End of the Day *By Tamar Frankiel, PhD, and Judy Greenfeld*
7 x 10, 192 pp, illus., Quality PB, 978-1-58023-079-7 **$16.95**

First Steps to a New Jewish Spirit: Reb Zalman's Guide to Recapturing the Intimacy & Ecstasy in Your Relationship with God *By Rabbi Zalman M. Schachter-Shalomi with Donald Gropman* 6 x 9, 144 pp, Quality PB, 978-1-58023-182-4 **$16.95**

Foundations of Sephardic Spirituality: The Inner Life of Jews of the Ottoman Empire
By Rabbi Marc D. Angel, PhD 6 x 9, 224 pp, Quality PB, 978-1-58023-341-5 **$18.99**

God & the Big Bang: Discovering Harmony between Science & Spirituality
By Dr. Daniel C. Matt 6 x 9, 216 pp, Quality PB, 978-1-879045-89-7 **$18.99**

God in Our Relationships: Spirituality between People from the Teachings of Martin Buber *By Rabbi Dennis S. Ross* 5½ x 8½, 160 pp, Quality PB, 978-1-58023-147-3 **$16.95**

Judaism, Physics and God: Searching for Sacred Metaphors in a Post-Einstein World
By Rabbi David W. Nelson 6 x 9, 352 pp, Quality PB, inc. reader's discussion guide,
978-1-58023-306-4 **$18.99**; HC, 352 pp, 978-1-58023-252-4 **$24.99**

Meaning & Mitzvah: Daily Practices for Reclaiming Judaism through Prayer, God, Torah, Hebrew, Mitzvot and Peoplehood *By Rabbi Goldie Milgram*
7 x 9, 336 pp, Quality PB, 978-1-58023-256-2 **$19.99**

Repentance: The Meaning and Practice of Teshuvah
By Dr. Louis E. Newman; Foreword by Rabbi Harold M. Schulweis; Preface by Rabbi Karyn D. Kedar
6 x 9, 256 pp, HC, 978-1-58023-426-9 **$24.99** Quality PB, 978-1-58023-718-5 **$18.99**

The Sabbath Soul: Mystical Reflections on the Transformative Power of Holy Time
Selection, Translation and Commentary by Eitan Fishbane, PhD
6 x 9, 208 pp, Quality PB, 978-1-58023-459-7 **$18.99**

Tanya, the Masterpiece of Hasidic Wisdom: Selections Annotated & Explained
Translation & Annotation by Rabbi Rami Shapiro; Foreword by Rabbi Zalman M. Schachter-Shalomi
5½ x 8½, 240 pp, Quality PB, 978-1-59473-275-1 **$16.99**

These Are the Words, 2nd Edition: A Vocabulary of Jewish Spiritual Life
By Rabbi Arthur Green, PhD 6 x 9, 320 pp, Quality PB, 978-1-58023-494-8 **$19.99**

Spirituality / Prayer

Davening: A Guide to Meaningful Jewish Prayer
By Rabbi Zalman Schachter-Shalomi with Joel Segel; Foreword by Rabbi Lawrence Kushner
A fresh approach to prayer for all who wish to appreciate the power of prayer's poetry, song and ritual, and to join the age-old conversation that Jews have had with God. 6 x 9, 240 pp, Quality PB, 978-1-58023-627-0 **$18.99**

Jewish Men Pray: Words of Yearning, Praise, Petition, Gratitude and Wonder from Traditional and Contemporary Sources
Edited by Rabbi Kerry M. Olitzky and Stuart M. Matlins; Foreword by Rabbi Bradley Shavit Artson, DHL
A celebration of Jewish men's voices in prayer—to strengthen, heal, comfort, and inspire—from the ancient world up to our own day.
5 x 7¼, 400 pp, HC, 978-1-58023-628-7 **$19.99**

Making Prayer Real: Leading Jewish Spiritual Voices on Why Prayer Is Difficult and What to Do about It *By Rabbi Mike Comins* 6 x 9, 320 pp, Quality PB, 978-1-58023-417-7 **$18.99**

Witnesses to the One: The Spiritual History of the *Sh'ma*
By Rabbi Joseph B. Meszler; Foreword by Rabbi Elyse Goldstein
6 x 9, 176 pp, Quality PB, 978-1-58023-400-9 **$16.99**; HC, 978-1-58023-309-5 **$19.99**

My People's Prayer Book Series: Traditional Prayers, Modern Commentaries *Edited by Rabbi Lawrence A. Hoffman, PhD*
Provides diverse and exciting commentary to the traditional liturgy. Will help you find new wisdom in Jewish prayer, and bring liturgy into your life. Each book includes Hebrew text, modern translations and commentaries from all perspectives of the Jewish world.

Vol. 1—The *Sh'ma* and Its Blessings
  7 x 10, 168 pp, HC, 978-1-879045-79-8 **$29.99**
Vol. 2—The *Amidah* 7 x 10, 240 pp, HC, 978-1-879045-80-4 **$24.95**
Vol. 3—*P'sukei D'zimrah* (Morning Psalms)
  7 x 10, 240 pp, HC, 978-1-879045-81-1 **$29.99**
Vol. 4—*Seder K'riat Hatorah* (The Torah Service)
  7 x 10, 264 pp, HC, 978-1-879045-82-8 **$29.99**
Vol. 5—*Birkhot Hashachar* (Morning Blessings)
  7 x 10, 240 pp, HC, 978-1-879045-83-5 **$24.95**
Vol. 6—*Tachanun* and Concluding Prayers
  7 x 10, 240 pp, HC, 978-1-879045-84-2 **$24.95**
Vol. 7—Shabbat at Home 7 x 10, 240 pp, HC, 978-1-879045-85-9 **$24.95**
Vol. 8—*Kabbalat Shabbat* (Welcoming Shabbat in the Synagogue)
  7 x 10, 240 pp, HC, 978-1-58023-121-3 **$24.99**
Vol. 9—Welcoming the Night: *Minchah* and *Ma'ariv* (Afternoon and
  Evening Prayer) 7 x 10, 272 pp, HC, 978-1-58023-262-3 **$24.99**
Vol. 10—Shabbat Morning: *Shacharit* and *Musaf* (Morning and
  Additional Services) 7 x 10, 240 pp, HC, 978-1-58023-240-1 **$29.99**

Spirituality / Lawrence Kushner

I'm God; You're Not: Observations on Organized Religion & Other Disguises of the Ego
  6 x 9, 256 pp, Quality PB, 978-1-58023-513-6 **$18.99**; HC, 978-1-58023-441-2 **$21.99**

The Book of Letters: A Mystical Hebrew Alphabet
  Popular HC Edition, 6 x 9, 80 pp, 2-color text, 978-1-879045-00-2 **$24.95**
  Collector's Limited Edition, 9 x 12, 80 pp, gold-foil-embossed pages, w/ limited-edition silkscreened
  print, 978-1-879045-04-0 **$349.00**

The Book of Miracles: A Young Person's Guide to Jewish Spiritual Awareness
  6 x 9, 96 pp, 2-color illus., HC, 978-1-879045-78-1 **$16.95** *For ages 9–13*

God Was in This Place & I, i Did Not Know: Finding Self, Spirituality and
  Ultimate Meaning 6 x 9, 192 pp, Quality PB, 978-1-879045-33-0 **$16.95**

Honey from the Rock: An Introduction to Jewish Mysticism
  6 x 9, 176 pp, Quality PB, 978-1-58023-073-5 **$16.95**

Invisible Lines of Connection: Sacred Stories of the Ordinary
  5½ x 8½, 160 pp, Quality PB, 978-1-879045-98-9 **$16.99**

The Way Into Jewish Mystical Tradition
  6 x 9, 224 pp, Quality PB, 978-1-58023-200-5 **$18.99**; HC, 978-1-58023-029-2 **$21.95**

Inspiration

Saying No and Letting Go: Jewish Wisdom on Making Room for What Matters Most
By Rabbi Edwin Goldberg, DHL; Foreword by Rabbi Naomi Levy
Taps into timeless Jewish wisdom that teaches how to "hold on tightly" to the things that matter most while learning to "let go lightly" of the demands and worries that do not ultimately matter. 6 x 9, 192 pp, Quality PB, 978-1-58023-670-6 **$16.99**

The Magic of Hebrew Chant: Healing the Spirit, Transforming the Mind, Deepening Love *By Rabbi Shefa Gold; Foreword by Sylvia Boorstein*
Introduces this transformative spiritual practice as a way to unlock the power of sacred texts and make prayer and meditation the delight of your life. Includes musical notations. 6 x 9, 352 pp, Quality PB, 978-1-58023-671-3 **$24.99**

The Bridge to Forgiveness: Stories and Prayers for Finding God and Restoring Wholeness *By Rabbi Karyn D. Kedar* 6 x 9, 176 pp, Quality PB, 978-1-58023-451-1 **$16.99**

The Empty Chair: Finding Hope and Joy—Timeless Wisdom from a Hasidic Master, Rebbe Nachman of Breslov *Adapted by Moshe Mykoff and the Breslov Research Institute*
4 x 6, 128 pp, Deluxe PB w/ flaps, 978-1-879045-67-5 **$9.99**

A Formula for Proper Living: Practical Lessons from Life and Torah
By Rabbi Abraham J. Twerski, MD 6 x 9, 144 pp, HC, 978-1-58023-402-3 **$19.99**

The Gentle Weapon: Prayers for Everyday and Not-So-Everyday Moments—Timeless Wisdom from the Teachings of the Hasidic Master, Rebbe Nachman of Breslov *Adapted by Moshe Mykoff and S. C. Mizrahi, together with the Breslov Research Institute*
4 x 6, 144 pp, Deluxe PB w/ flaps, 978-1-58023-022-3 **$9.99**

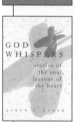

The God Upgrade: Finding Your 21st-Century Spirituality in Judaism's 5,000-Year-Old Tradition *By Rabbi Jamie Korngold; Foreword by Rabbi Harold M. Schulweis*
6 x 9, 176 pp, Quality PB, 978-1-58023-443-6 $15.99

God Whispers: Stories of the Soul, Lessons of the Heart *By Rabbi Karyn D. Kedar*
6 x 9, 176 pp, Quality PB, 978-1-58023-088-9 **$15.95**

God's To-Do List: 103 Ways to Be an Angel and Do God's Work on Earth
By Dr. Ron Wolfson 6 x 9, 144 pp, Quality PB, 978-1-58023-301-9 **$16.99**

Happiness and the Human Spirit: The Spirituality of Becoming the Best You Can Be
By Rabbi Abraham J. Twerski, MD
6 x 9, 176 pp, Quality PB, 978-1-58023-404-7 **$16.99**; HC, 978-1-58023-343-9 **$19.99**

Life's Daily Blessings: Inspiring Reflections on Gratitude and Joy for Every Day, Based on Jewish Wisdom *By Rabbi Kerry M. Olitzky* 4½ x 6½, 368 pp, Quality PB, 978-1-58023-396-5 **$16.99**

Restful Reflections: Nighttime Inspiration to Calm the Soul, Based on Jewish Wisdom
By Rabbi Kerry M. Olitzky and Rabbi Lori Forman-Jacobi 5 x 8, 352 pp, Quality PB, 978-1-58023-091-9 **$16.99**

Sacred Intentions: Morning Inspiration to Strengthen the Spirit, Based on Jewish Wisdom
By Rabbi Kerry M. Olitzky and Rabbi Lori Forman-Jacobi 4½ x 6½, 448 pp, Quality PB, 978-1-58023-061-2 **$16.99**

The Seven Questions You're Asked in Heaven: Reviewing and Renewing Your Life on Earth *By Dr. Ron Wolfson* 6 x 9, 176 pp, Quality PB, 978-1-58023-407-8 **$16.99**

Kabbalah / Mysticism

Jewish Mysticism and the Spiritual Life: Classical Texts, Contemporary Reflections *Edited by Dr. Lawrence Fine, Dr. Eitan Fishbane and Rabbi Or N. Rose*
Inspirational and thought-provoking materials for contemplation, discussion and action. 6 x 9, 256 pp, HC, 978-1-58023-434-4 **$24.99** Quality PB, 978-1-58023-719-2 **$18.99**

Ehyeh: A Kabbalah for Tomorrow
By Rabbi Arthur Green, PhD 6 x 9, 224 pp, Quality PB, 978-1-58023-213-5 **$18.99**

The Gift of Kabbalah: Discovering the Secrets of Heaven, Renewing Your Life on Earth
By Tamar Frankiel, PhD 6 x 9, 256 pp, Quality PB, 978-1-58023-141-1 **$16.95**

Seek My Face: A Jewish Mystical Theology *By Rabbi Arthur Green, PhD*
6 x 9, 304 pp, Quality PB, 978-1-58023-130-5 **$19.95**

Zohar: Annotated & Explained *Translation & Annotation by Dr. Daniel C. Matt; Foreword by Andrew Harvey* 5½ x 8½, 176 pp, Quality PB, 978-1-893361-51-5 **$16.99**
(A book from SkyLight Paths, Jewish Lights' sister imprint)

See also *The Way Into Jewish Mystical Tradition* in The Way Into... Series.

Theology / Philosophy

From Defender to Critic: The Search for a New Jewish Self
By Dr. David Hartman
A daring self-examination of Hartman's goals, which were not to strip halakha of its authority but to create a space for questioning and critique that allows for the traditionally religious Jew to act out a moral life in tune with modern experience.
6 x 9, 336 pp, HC, 978-1-58023-515-0 **$35.00**

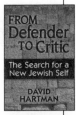

The God Who Hates Lies: Confronting & Rethinking Jewish Tradition
A deeply personal look at the struggle between commitment to Jewish religious tradition and personal morality.
By Dr. David Hartman with Charlie Buckholtz 6 x 9, 208 pp, HC, 978-1-58023-455-9 **$24.99**

Our Religious Brains: What Cognitive Science Reveals about Belief, Morality, Community and Our Relationship with God
By Rabbi Ralph D. Mecklenburger; Foreword by Dr. Howard Kelfer; Preface by Dr. Neil Gillman
This is a groundbreaking, accessible look at the implications of cognitive science for religion and theology, intended for laypeople. 6 x 9, 224 pp, HC, 978-1-58023-508-2 **$24.99**

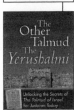

The Other Talmud—*The Yerushalmi*: Unlocking the Secrets of The Talmud of Israel for Judaism Today *By Rabbi Judith Z. Abrams, PhD*
A fascinating—and stimulating—look at "the other Talmud" and the possibilities for Jewish life reflected there. 6 x 9, 256 pp, HC, 978-1-58023-463-4 **$24.99**

The Way of Man: According to Hasidic Teaching
By Martin Buber; New Translation and Introduction by Rabbi Bernard H. Mehlman and Dr. Gabriel E. Padawer; Foreword by Paul Mendes-Flohr
An accessible and engaging new translation of Buber's classic work—*available as an e-book only.* E-book, 978-1-58023-601-0 Digital List Price **$14.99**

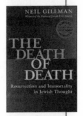

The Death of Death: Resurrection and Immortality in Jewish Thought
By Rabbi Neil Gillman, PhD 6 x 9, 336 pp, Quality PB, 978-1-58023-081-0 **$18.95**

Doing Jewish Theology: God, Torah & Israel in Modern Judaism *By Rabbi Neil Gillman, PhD*
6 x 9, 304 pp, Quality PB, 978-1-58023-439-9 **$18.99**; HC, 978-1-58023-322-4 **$24.99**

A Heart of Many Rooms: Celebrating the Many Voices within Judaism
By Dr. David Hartman 6 x 9, 352 pp, Quality PB, 978-1-58023-156-5 **$19.95**

Jewish Theology in Our Time: A New Generation Explores the Foundations and Future of Jewish Belief *Edited by Rabbi Elliot J. Cosgrove, PhD; Foreword by Rabbi David J. Wolpe; Preface by Rabbi Carole B. Balin, PhD* 6 x 9, 240 pp, Quality PB, 978-1-58023-630-1, **$19.99**; HC, 978-1-58023-413-9 **$24.99**

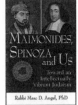

Maimonides—Essential Teachings on Jewish Faith & Ethics: The Book of Knowledge & the Thirteen Principles of Faith—Annotated & Explained
Translation and Annotation by Rabbi Marc D. Angel, PhD
5½ x 8½, 224 pp, Quality PB Original, 978-1-59473-311-6 **$18.99***

Maimonides, Spinoza and Us: Toward an Intellectually Vibrant Judaism
By Rabbi Marc D. Angel, PhD 6 x 9, 224 pp, HC, 978-1-58023-411-5 **$24.99**

Your Word Is Fire: The Hasidic Masters on Contemplative Prayer
Edited and translated by Rabbi Arthur Green, PhD, and Barry W. Holtz
6 x 9, 160 pp, Quality PB, 978-1-879045-25-5 **$16.99**

I Am Jewish
Personal Reflections Inspired by the Last Words of Daniel Pearl
Almost 150 Jews—both famous and not—from all walks of life, from all around the world, write about many aspects of their Judaism.
Edited by Judea and Ruth Pearl 6 x 9, 304 pp, Deluxe PB w/ flaps, 978-1-58023-259-3 **$19.99**
Download a free copy of the *I Am Jewish Teacher's Guide* at www.jewishlights.com.

Hannah Senesh: Her Life and Diary, The First Complete Edition
By Hannah Senesh; Foreword by Marge Piercy; Preface by Eitan Senesh; Afterword by Roberta Grossman
6 x 9, 368 pp, b/w photos, Quality PB, 978-1-58023-342-2 **$19.99**

**A book from SkyLight Paths, Jewish Lights' sister imprint*

About Jewish Lights

People of all faiths and backgrounds yearn for books that attract, engage, educate, and spiritually inspire.

Our principal goal is to stimulate thought and help all people learn about who the Jewish People are, where they come from, and what the future can be made to hold. While people of our diverse Jewish heritage are the primary audience, our books speak to people in the Christian world as well and will broaden their understanding of Judaism and the roots of their own faith.

We bring to you authors who are at the forefront of spiritual thought and experience. While each has something different to say, they all say it in a voice that you can hear.

Our books are designed to welcome you and then to engage, stimulate, and inspire. We judge our success not only by whether or not our books are beautiful and commercially successful, but by whether or not they make a difference in your life.

For your information and convenience, at the back of this book we have provided a list of other Jewish Lights books you might find interesting and useful. They cover all the categories of your life:

Bar/Bat Mitzvah	Life Cycle
Bible Study / Midrash	Meditation
Children's Books	Men's Interest
Congregation Resources	Parenting
Current Events / History	Prayer / Ritual / Sacred Practice
Ecology / Environment	Social Justice
Fiction: Mystery, Science Fiction	Spirituality
Grief / Healing	Theology / Philosophy
Holidays / Holy Days	Travel
Inspiration	Twelve Steps
Kabbalah / Mysticism / Enneagram	Women's Interest

Stuart M. Matlins, Publisher

Or phone, fax, mail or e-mail to: **JEWISH LIGHTS Publishing**
Sunset Farm Offices, Route 4 • P.O. Box 237 • Woodstock, Vermont 05091
Tel: (802) 457-4000 • Fax: (802) 457-4004 • www.jewishlights.com
Credit card orders: (800) 962-4544 (8:30AM–5:30PM EST Monday–Friday)
Generous discounts on quantity orders. SATISFACTION GUARANTEED. Prices subject to change.

**For more information about each book,
visit our website at www.jewishlights.com**